The SECRET OF GOD

The SECRET OF GOD

LINDA MCCLARY MARTIN

Crossover

The Secret of God

By: Linda McClary Martin

Published by:
Crossover Publications LLC
870 N. Bierdeman Road
Pearl, Mississippi 39208
www.crossoverpublications.com
Phone: (601) 664-6717, Fax: (601) 664-6818

ISBN 978-0-9819657-3-4

Printed in the USA

Cover Concept and Artwork: Randall M. Mooney
Cover Graphics and Design: R. Matthew Mooney

Table of Contents

Acknowledgements

First, I want to thank my husband, Leonard, for the time this took away from him; for believing in me and encouraging me. You are my dearest friend.

Second, I want to thank my friend, teacher, mentor, and coach, Gay Bissell. You have taught me well, built me up and spent many hours in prayer for me. Bless you!

Finally, many heart-felt thanks to Kay Morgan. Kay read, re-read, corrected and aided in this manuscript above and beyond the call of duty. Thank you, precious friend!

Dedication

This work is dedicated to my first love.

Nevertheless I have somewhat against thee, because thou hast left thy first love. – Rev. 2:4 (KJV)

I have heard and read this scripture over the years and I understood "first love" to mean, "The one I love the most" or "The one I *should* love the most" or "The one I once loved the most". Naturally, God wants to be and should be the first and most important one I love. I hope this is true for me, and it has become a subject of my thoughts recently, bringing me to a new perspective on this scripture – let me tell you about it.

Several months ago I was introduced to a music CD called *Eternity* by Jo Ann McFadder. She sings about eternity being the place where God lives and views everything. Layer on that a teaching I heard about the same time, expressing that God is not confined by time or space – from where He sits He can see the past and the future as if it were now. When God intervenes in our now, He does it from eternity. I have meditated quite a lot on this concept recently . . . then I remembered this scripture:

> *For you formed my inward parts; you wove me in my mother's womb. I will give thanks to you, for I am fearfully and wonderfully made; wonderful are your works, and my soul knows it very well. My frame was not hidden from you, when I was made in secret, and skillfully wrought in the depths of the earth; your eyes have seen my unformed substance; and in your book were all written the days that were ordained for me, when as yet there was not one of them.* Psalm 139:13-16 (NIV)

Finally, another song I listen to often calls Him the *"lover of my soul."* All these merged to build this new perspective – my newest *aha* moment.

He knew me first,
He loved me first – before anyone loved me,
He loved me and I loved Him – before I loved anyone
I loved Him! He really is my first love.

As I write this, I am reminded that as a child I would tell Him good night and blow Him a kiss before going to sleep. I remember quiet summer days lying in the cool clover of the schoolyard behind my house, I would look up into the sky wishing I could fly away to play with Him.

Those feelings cooled over the years to the point that I began to believe He was not a caring God, didn't know me personally and didn't care to know me. Fortunately, He didn't leave me in that state. He moved from eternity into my now and made Himself known to me one afternoon in 1980 in my son's bedroom. His Love, His Glory and His Hope filled my life.

I cannot turn my back on that kind of love. This is the kind of love that builds confidence in His goodness and faithfulness. He knows me, He remembers me, He watched me grow up and He loved me all along the way. This book and my life are dedicated to My First Love.

Nevertheless, I have somewhat against thee, because thou hast left thy first love. Rev. 2:4 (KJV)

Purpose

My purpose is to introduce you to the creative life you were destined for and the source of the power to live this life to the fullest with the greatest of success. Creativity, creative ideas, desires, and destiny were placed in us when He created us. Many lay dormant waiting for the right conditions to launch into life. This creativity and destiny is in seed form, embedded in the DNA of who we are as individuals. Can these seeds lay dormant in our lives? Yes, but sometimes they are waiting for proper conditions. Sometimes they come to life because the proper timing has been filled.

I looked up "Seed Dormancy" and found it defined as a state in which seeds are prevented from germinating even under environmental conditions normally favorable for germination. Most of us have been exposed to good academics, loving mentors, and multiple types of media – so the environmental conditions are favorable for creativity and success – right? So where is that whole, abundant, and powerful life? You will find in these pages the ingredients needed to begin seeing real creativity in your life.

The life God desires for each of us can be accomplished and become as natural as breathing when we partner with Him. My hope, in the following pages, is that you find and put into practice the steps to living a supernatural life in this natural world. Then my prayer is that you take the supernatural life you gain and create a revolution in the world you occupy – and perhaps occupy more territory.

I'm not introducing a new doctrine or discipline. I simply wish to express the ease of living in the fullness of His creative life. The life I am about to introduce comes from my experience as a Christian. Becoming a Christian infused my spirit with life and gave me a direct wireless connection to God's Spirit. This Spirit-to-spirit connection empowers me to accomplish the supernatural in this natural realm.

In my preparation of this text, I was directed by Holy Spirit to read the fourth chapter of every one of the Apostle Paul's letters. I sensed He wanted me to read and re-read those chapters until I could boil them down to one core, power verse from each chapter. An unusual request, I thought; why the fourth chapter? In an attempt to answer that question, I researched the significance of FOUR as it relates to Scripture. My quest eventually took me to "Number in Scripture".[1]

There I learned: **Four is the number for creation (imagine that?).** For example:

> *Now the number four is made up of three and one* (3+1=4), *and it denotes, therefore, and marks that which follows the revelation of God, namely, His creative works. He is known by the things that are seen. Hence the written revelation commences with the words, In-the-beginning God CREATED. Creation is therefore the next thing—the fourth thing, and the number four always has reference to all that is created. It is emphatically the number of Creation.*
> *The fourth day saw the material creation finished (for on the fifth and sixth days it was only the furnishing and peopling of the earth with living creatures). The sun, moon, and stars completed the work, and they were to give light upon the earth which had been created, and to rule over the day and over the night (Gen 1:14-19).*

- *Four is the number of the great elements—earth, air, fire, and water.*
- *Four are the regions of the earth—north, south, east, and west.*
- *Four are the divisions of the day—morning, noon, evening, and midnight. Or in our Lord's words, when He speaks of His coming at evening, midnight, cock crowing, or in the morning (Mark 13:35). We are never to put off His coming in our minds beyond tomorrow morning.*

---

1 Number in Scripture: Its Supernatural Design and Spiritual Significance by Ethelbert W. Bullinger

- *Four are the seasons of the year—spring, summer, autumn, and winter.*
- *Four are the great variations of the lunar phases."*

Four is the number of creation, creativity, and life. That is the central theme of this book and Holy Spirit's purpose in my writing it. Our precious Lord Jesus is partnering, Spirit-to-Spirit, with His twenty-first century church to co-create a life that is creative, wondrous, victorious, genuine, and will impact our world for His Kingdom. He wants to bring Heaven to earth; He wants His Kingdom to be established on earth, as it is in heaven. We are His people, called by His Name (Christian), set apart to influence and establish in the world around us all the abundance of His mighty kingdom. Make no mistake, He is ready to set you free so you can arise and shine.

At the end of this book, you will find each of the core scriptures from each of the fourth chapters of Paul's letters, in book order. I encourage you to memorize them, speak them into the atmosphere of your home, your car, your work place, your classroom, and your church. Walk your neighborhood and proclaim them. It is the Word of God and **"it is living"!**

THE DEPOSIT

Within you, the Lord has made a deposit of creativity that will provide for all your needs and wants. We need to dig in, dig down, and find it! Do not dismiss this idea by saying, *"I can't, I don't have, I always fail."* In God's plan and His economy for you, "I can't" and "I don't have" are not in His vocabulary; why is it part of ours?

He wants us to develop and live in a spirit of expectation of good and positive, not negative – never negative. Your beliefs about yourself are negative. They are not in agreement with His beliefs about you. Further, what you believe becomes a magnet. What do you want to attract with this magnet? Move from worry to worship. Let Him empower you to be grateful, to forgive, release, BELIEVE.

He formed you in the dark, before you existed physically. You are His – give birth to the life He placed in you. He wants you to believe Him and agree with Him, not just believe *in Him*.

Yes, I said He made a deposit of creativity in you; I did not say He placed a deposit of creativity in you. There is a difference in these two words, but you might think they are the same. It is a part of who you are, not something separate that was later added.

TRUSTED SERVANTS

I AM A FRIEND OF GOD

God, the Creator of all we see and all we cannot see; the One who spoke and it was; the One who parted the sea so the slaves of Egypt could escape their captors; the one who opened blind eyes, blessed children and rebuked devils; to see Him is sure death. Yes, that very One, can we be friends? I believe so. In order for us to explore this possibility, let us look at some close relationships that may allow our logical mind the opportunity to wrap itself around this concept.

According to the Bible and the testimony of contemporary men and women, God is in relationship with His creation in various levels and degrees. Let us take a look at three types of relationships within our realm of understanding.

1) CHILD: A person born into or adopted by a family.

All of us have been a child; some of us have had a child. The dynamics of this relationship range from healthy to malignant. Translating this to a Parent/child relationship with God can be a stretch for some of us. Let us begin this relationship view by finding out what the Bible has to say on the subject.

In the New Testament, followers of Christ are referred to as "children of **light**" (Luke 16:8; 1 Thess. 5:5) and "children of **obedience**" (1 Peter 1:14). That can sound so ethereal until you put it into context of who He is. In 1 John 1:5 the Bible says, "*This then is the message which we have heard of him* [Jesus], *and declare unto you, that God is **light**. . .*" (KJV) If indeed God is light then we, as His followers, are called "children of light." It seems a stretch to go from follower or believer to child. What has happened to cause us to be related as child? Could our belief alone be enough to create the Parent/child relationship?

In Hebrews 3:18-19 when referring to the children of Israel in the wilderness, the Bible says, *"And to whom did he make an oath that they might not come into his rest? Was it not to those who went against his orders? So we see that they were not able to go in because they had no belief."* (*BBE*) This word (no belief) unbelief is translated from the Hebrew word, *apaistia* (ap-is-tee'-ah) meaning faithlessness, disbelief, or unfaithfulness, **disobedience.**

So, being a child of obedience is to believe and be obedient to God. It is not enough to believe; one must translate that belief into obedience. Obedience would be difficult for those of us who have experienced a harsh parent or harsh authorities. However, God is not about developing relationship with us on this basis. Believing and obedience still is not enough to translate us into the Parent/child relationship with God.

In the letter written by James (2:19) it says, *"Thou believest that there is one God; thou doest well: the devils also believe, and tremble."* (KJV) In Mark 1:27 the Bible also says that the spirits obey Him (referring to Jesus). The spirits believe and obey; we believe and obey.

What would be the missing ingredient in this relationship between mankind becoming a child and devils merely knowing, believing, obeying and trembling? I deem it is found in the discourse Jesus had with Nicodemus in the Gospel of John, chapter 3: That which is born of flesh is flesh; that which is born of spirit is spirit; you must be born again (my paraphrase). To become a Christian you must be born into it – thereby becoming a child. *"And* (I) *will be a Father unto you, and ye shall be my sons and daughters, saith the Lord Almighty."* 2 Cor. 6:18 (KJV)

In an extremely well written reference Bible, researched by Fennis J. Dake, Dake expresses the Parent/child relationship to God referencing this scripture thusly, *"The same kind of promise as 2 Sam. 7:14, this means that God will assume all responsibility of parental concern and give Himself to the eternal care of His family* (Eph.3:14; Matt. 7:11). *Earthly parents may lack the power and means to supply all things for their families, but this is not true of God who owns all and rules all."* © 1961, 1989

Everything God does is accomplished in two realms. Whatever is done here in the earthly or natural realm is first done in the heavenly or super-natural realm. Matt: 6:10 says, *"Thy kingdom come, Thy will be done, in earth, as it is in heaven."* (KJV) This is also true with birth; we conceive and give birth to a baby, but the child's life comes straight from the heavenly realm. The second birth, the birth Jesus discussed with Nicodemus, is also a Spirit realm to natural realm transference. <u>This change begins within our spirit, translating into our whole life.</u> Remember this last sentence; we will discuss its importance in each following chapter.

2) SERVANT or REPRESENTATIVE

To be a servant or representative of God is not too much to comprehend for most of us since we consider ourselves a servant (or employee) on some level and are familiar with the operational concept in our daily lives. Likewise, we are accustomed to organizational charts and levels of authority in school, work, military and civic organizations. Some of us have even been involved in organizations where secrets are held up as something we protect, such as a Top Secret clearance in the military, a non-compete or non-disclosure clause in our employment contracts or fraternal organizations. What does the Bible say about this relationship?

Paul introduced himself by this role in Rom 1:1 (KJV), *"Paul, a servant of Jesus Christ..."* and in I Cor. 1:1 (KJV), *"Paul, called to be an apostle of Jesus Christ..."* and in Phil. 1:1, *"Paul and Timotheus, the servants of Jesus Christ..."* An ambassador or representative in the Old Testament Hebrew word *tsir*, meant "one who goes on an errand." It is rendered thus (Josh 9:4; Prov. 13:17; Isa. 18:2; Jer. 49:14; Obad. 1) ...meaning "an interpreter" (2 Chron. 32:31) ...or a "messenger" (2 Chronicles 35:21; Isa. 30:4; 33:7; Ezek. 17:15). This is the name used by the Apostle Paul as designating those who are appointed by God to declare his will (2 Cor. 5:20; Eph 6:20). To do injury to an ambassador was to insult the king who sent him (2 Sam 10:5). *(Easton's Bible Dictionary, PC Study Bible formatted electronic database Copyright © 2003, 2006 Biblesoft, Inc. All rights reserved.)*

We have the ability to understand the relationship position of someone who is working for God, like the apostle Paul, our local pastors or even the current Pope. However, I do not believe God views this relationship as a career choice. I am fully persuaded that to represent God one must actually go into His presence to hear what He is saying. I fully believe God is talking; He has much to say and very few are listening. The apostle Paul did not write all the wonderful letters in the New Testament solely based on his memory of the Old Testament. He took the truth he knew from the Word of God, spent time in prayer and meditation, and allowed the character of God to develop within him and translate into the words of these living epistles.

In my many years of employment, I have had the privilege of working under the leadership of men and women of excellent character. They led by inspiration and impartation, which left them with a well trained, well-developed and devoted staff. It has been my experience with God, as we co-labor, that He wants me to do well, as it reflects more precisely and positively on Him and on what He is about. God is a benevolent mentor, not a religious dictator. Being His servant, co-laborer, or any position He assigns me is easy as long as I am willing to be led. He will supply all I need for the job.

3) FRIEND

Real, genuine, close friends know each other well; they know each other's weaknesses, strengths and secrets. Their relationship is ongoing and cherished. To become friends, we must invest time in each other: time that develops trust, time that develops a bond. Friendship is the top of the relationship chain. It is the ultimate goal of all relationships (Parent/child, employer/employee, husband/wife, God/mankind) because of the level of trust developed over time. It is God's purpose in creation (see Genesis 1 and 2). God created, gave dominion of the created world to His creation (man) and came to walk with Adam and Eve in the cool of the day. God has not changed in His desire to have relationship with His creation. If we are in relationship with Him, then we are His trusted servants, but more – He calls us friend, brother and child.

Other examples of friends of God in the Bible:

- Abraham is called "God's friend forever" (II Chronicles 20:11, Isaiah 41:8 and James 2:23).
- God spoke face-to-face with Moses as a man speaks to a friend (Exodus 33:11).
- David is called *"a man after Mine own heart, which shall fulfill all my will."* Acts 13:22 (KJV)
- God's obvious motive in rescuing the descendants of Israel (Jacob) from the bondage of the Egyptian ruler was relationship. *"And they shall know that I am the Lord their God, that brought them forth out of the land of Egypt, that I may dwell among them: I am the Lord their God."* (Ex. 29:46) emphasis mine

God desires friendship with us. He knows all about us and He wants us to know Him. He wants to call us "beloved friend and precious child." Unfortunately, most of us are mere acquaintances of God or worse, know about Him but never know Him.

Secrets, Just Between Friends

God has secrets; however, His are not like CIA-type classified secrets, but they are character qualities only known to close friends. We each have qualities, gifts and abilities that are secret to all except those who know us and are, on some level, in relationship with us. You can know about me, but to truly experience me you must get to know me. You can read the Bible and know about God and the people He had relationships with, but still never know Him. Worse still, you can be born again and let that be the end of your quest.

Our Bible confirms God's secrets and His desire to share them:

> *So then, men ought to regard us as* SERVANTS *of Christ and as* ***those entrusted*** *with the* **secret** *things of God.* I Corinthians 4:1 (NIV, emphasis mine)

> *The* **secret** *[of the sweet, satisfying companionship] of the Lord have they who fear (revere and worship) Him, and He will show them His covenant and reveal to them its [deep, inner] meaning.* Psalm 25:14 (Amplified, emphasis mine)

> The translation of Psalm 25:14 in the KJV is like this: *"The Secret of the Lord is with them that fear Him; and He will show them His covenant."*

> *You are my friends if you do what I command you. No longer do I call you slaves, for the slave does not know what his master is doing; but I have called you friends, for all things that I have heard from My Father I have made known to you.* John 15:14-15 (NAS)

The benefits of this close relationship are endless: He is our comforter, our advocate, the one who redeems us (buys our freedom from slavery to self-medication, self-centeredness, logic, reason, and brokenness. . .) He is our wisdom, our portion, our provision, our healer, our righteous judge, our ever-present help in time of need, our connection to the creative, and so much more. His secrets (character qualities) have a dimension of power, authority and liberty that are transferable to His friends. This power is His Grace. It is available through His Holy Spirit to enable you and me to do *"all things through Christ. . ."* (Phil. 4:13).

Can we really have such an intimate relationship with God? Is it possible to know Him and not just know about him? **ABSOLUTELY!**

> Jesus said, *"Do not hold on to me, for I have not yet returned to the Father. Go instead to my* ***brothers*** *and tell them, 'I am returning to my Father and* ***your Father****, to my God and* ***your God****.'"* John 20:17 (NIV)

We have available to us the extravagant opportunity to get to know Him and actually become His friend. In the process of knowing Him we have the added opportunity to become all that He created us to be. As the creator of all things, we His friend, can partner with Him to change the corner of the world He placed us in – the work product of this friendship.

In this ongoing relationship He will teach us to see ourselves the way He sees us; we will develop our identification in Him as His child, friend and servant. He is more actively committed to this relationship in that He supplies all we could ever need through a supernatural impartation. Our contribution is difficult at first, but easy in the long run – obedience and trust. Our obedience and trust become EASY because we discover His faithfulness and His love for us. It is not obedience to a hard task master or an untrustworthy companion.

There may be many times in the process where you say to yourself, "I cannot do this!" It is then we can remind ourselves that He is fully committed to us; He is committed to walking with us through the process. There is always progress in His process. He will show you how you CAN, and He will give you everything you need to succeed. He is committed to your prosperity: mentally, emotionally, physically, financially and spiritually. This relationship is all about success and positive growth; however, there will be times it won't necessarily feel like it. He will, however, supply all we need; He will finish the project of establishing us in wholeness, that we can become His partner in establishing His Kingdom on earth in the lives of others.

LET HIM – HE IS WORTHY OF TRUST: HE IS A FAITHFUL FRIEND

I have been in the process of developing this friend relationship with God since 1980. We have walked and talked together. He has brought incredible healing into my life and has answered many, many prayers. Because of this, I can say with confidence, He is worthy of your trust. You may not be willing to take my word alone for this; I completely understand. I have given a lot of thought to the concept of "worthy," and that kind of thinking usually takes me to the dictionary.

A combining form of worthy, occurring in adjectives that have the general sense "deserving of, fit for" (blameworthy; newsworthy; noteworthy; trustworthy), "capable of travel in or on" (airworthy; roadworthy; seaworthy), as specified by the first word of the compound.

Dictionary.com Unabridged Based on the Random House Dictionary
© Random House, Inc. 2009

Let us imagine together that you have a very long trip ahead of you. Your travel plans will require a great ship. How do you go about choosing a ship "worthy" of the trip? None of us would simply go out and purchase a ship on the word of someone we don't know unless they had direct experience and a documented history of the vessel. This vessel will need to carry your life and your cargo. You will need to be able to depend on the core structure of the vessel to take you through many different environments and conditions. You will want something seaworthy. What criteria do you use to determine worthiness? Four principal terms needed to describe a seaworthy performance are:

1. Mission: What the ship is intended to accomplish.

2. Environment: The conditions under which the ship is operating.
3. Ship responses: The response of the ship to the environmental conditions.
4. Seakeeping performance criteria: The established limits for the ship's responses. These are based on the ship motions and the accelerations…comfort…vibration…and bow immersion. Lewis, *Principals of Naval Architecture,* Volume III, Section 7, p. 137 (Measures of Performance).

My ability to say, "Let Him – He is Worthy of Trust," is based on my direct experience and my documented history. What other criteria do you need to determine His worthiness for the balance of your trip through this life? Would you need other direct experience and documentation? Certainly. The Bible is full of such material. Ask yourself, "what is my…"

1. Mission: What am I wanting to do, where am I headed?
2. Environment: What is ahead of me? Do I know, and can I control it?
3. Ship responses: Can He be depended on to hear me when I call?
4. Seakeeping performance criteria: Does He provide me with security and protection?

My answers to the above questions:

1. God has a purpose for you – are you headed in that direction (Jer. 29:11)?
2. No, we don't know the environment ahead of us, but He does (Isa. 46:10).

3. *"Call to Me and I will answer you, and I will tell you great and mighty things, which you do not know."* Jeremiah 33:3 (NAS)
4. Psalm 91

I keep a prayer list. Some items on my list seem to have taken up a permanent position. Because of this, I catch myself worrying over this list. Naturally, I want it done yesterday. His ways are higher than my ways, and His thoughts are higher than my thoughts (Isa. 55:9). I have learned that God is not a vending machine that spits out answered prayer. Some answered prayer is a process, while some is instant. All prayers however, must be acquired in the spirit realm before they are ever seen in this realm.

Recently, He asked me to commit that list to Him. That means that I cannot tell Him when, what or how to do it. He asked that I not focus on the problem or the future resolution but to focus on the hope of His plan. He has a plan and it is a very good plan. He has also asked me to open my mouth <u>in agreement to His plan</u>. It is a great waste of prayer if all I do is speak the problem.

> *What you say can mean life or death. Those who speak with care will be rewarded.* Proverbs 18:21 (New Century Version)

This was difficult for me. When I didn't see activity, I thought God had forgotten, the devil had gotten into the mix, and/or I wasn't doing something I needed to do to help HIM – like fasting, praising, or some other religious activity.

This is so not true. If God needs me TO DO something, He is well able to tell me and will enable me to do it. Faith says, "I will not look at the circumstances with my natural eyes – I will train myself to look from the perspective of the promises of God." I have to remind myself that I cannot pray with power, confidence and authority if I only look at what I see taking place around me. My new perspective is a result of reloading my mind with new, true information gained from The Word of God (Bible).

GOD'S PERFECT TIMING

Several years ago I worked with a precious Christian girl about my daughter's age. Her husband was in medical school to become a dentist. He is my dentist now. A year before he graduated, they started trying to get pregnant. They found that she had some serious problems, and was told she would likely not become pregnant. Nevertheless, they tried everything medical science had available. After thousands upon thousands upon thousands of dollars, much pain and many, many disappointments, they quit trying and shortly after adopted a little boy. Two years later they adopted another little boy. Then shortly afterward she had surgery and lost one of her ovaries. She was having serious hormone wars, so the doctor put her on the pill. I, and many others, prayed for her about three years until they decided to adopt. Each time I would go to the dentist, I would see pictures of their boys and how big and beautiful they were becoming.

On a recent visit after having my teeth cleaned, I stopped at the front desk to pay, and I saw the picture of a brand new baby and asked, "Who's baby?" The receptionist told me it was the doctor and his wife's third little boy. I understood her to tell me that two little boys were her limit, so I was surprised – and made the comment that I was surprised and asked when they had adopted him. The receptionist smiled and said, they didn't – she gave birth four weeks ago. God is worthy of our trust! One ovary and on the pill, but He answered all those prayers!

I am developing a determination to trust Him even if I don't see activity; especially when I don't SEE the changes I'm praying for. Each time one of the items from my list comes to mind, I am training myself to dismiss the instinct to worry, and simply thank Him. If it comes to mind several times in a day, I ask Him if there is something He wants me to do. If there is, I do IT; if not, I thank Him!

> *Trust in the LORD with all thine heart; and lean not unto thine own understanding. In all thy ways acknowledge Him, and He shall direct thy paths.* Proverbs 3:5-6 (KJV)

There are things on my prayer list that I have prayed over and over and over. He has asked me to lay them down and walk away from them so that when things are accomplished I will not be able to say I was instrumental in the outcome. That is easier said than done. If I refuse to let go, He will remove them from me, which He has done with a couple of them. At the time of this writing, all I have to go on is my faith in His faithfulness and His goodness. He has my list in one hand and with His other hand He carries me.

HISTORY WITH GOD – FRIENDSHIP DEVELOPMENT

We are often told that we cannot base our relationship with God on various significant experiences and/or miracles. In other words, we cannot live on today what He did for us yesterday. We are told we cannot save yesterday's manna, so to speak, to give us life today. Indeed this is true. However, it is yesterday's manna that got me to today. My relationship with my Lord isn't based (alone) on the fact that His mercy is new every morning, but is enhanced by my relationship history with Him. Relationship history is every bit as important as the new manna that is given for our growth and survival. It validates in our soul His faithfulness, His love, and the value He places on our lives. And day upon day it changes our perspective of the world and of ourselves.

To be clear, this relationship is NOT about things, but things are a natural byproduct. This relationship is NOT about signs and wonders, but they are the bells and whistles. This relationship IS about loving Him and allowing **His friendship and His Secret** to prosper us and empower us to Love, live in Unity, Forgive, understand and operate in Faith and Humility, change our Perspective in every situation, develop Gratitude, Generosity, Integrity and Honor.

These words are tossed about freely in the 21st century community. For many of us, they are just words with a benign hope attached, no real confidence that we will ever be able to develop these abilities. The Secret works because the creator established it. Actively, deliberately, EXPECT to produce in your life. My appeal through these next few pages is that we move from this benign hope toward grace (empowered hope) in the One who established this irreversible secret. The very One who creates and produces, through you, His plans and purposes and the abundant life Jesus PROMISED.

> *The thief comes only to steal and kill and destroy; I came that they may have life, and have it abundantly.*
> John 10:10 (NAS, emphasis mine)

Throughout this text I will be giving you scripture to read and memorize. I have only one purpose in so doing – you need it to survive, live, thrive and conquer. If you find any area of your life where you are weak or you feel needs to be developed – the Word of God is the tool for the task. Look up the scriptures, write them down on an index card, and put them in your pocket – read them several times a day – commit them to memory and meditate on them. Write them on your bathroom mirror with a dry erase pen so it will be the first and last thing you see, daily.

THE TRUTH ABOUT HOPE
Scriptures to Memorize (all NAS)*

*Be strong and let your heart take courage, all you who **hope** in the LORD.* (Psalm 31:24)

*Behold, the eye of the LORD is on those who fear Him, on those who **hope** for His lovingkindness. . .* (Psalm 33:18)

Let Your lovingkindness, O LORD, be upon us, According as we have ***hoped*** *in You.* (Psalm 33:22)

For I ***hope*** *in You, O LORD; You will answer, O Lord my God.* (Psalm 38:15)

And now, Lord, for what do I wait? My ***hope*** *is in You.* (Psalm 39:7)

Why are you in despair, O my soul? And why have you become disturbed within me? ***Hope*** *in God, for I shall again praise Him for the help of His presence.* (Psalm 42:5)

"For I know the plans that I have for you," declares the LORD, "plans for welfare and not for calamity to give you a future and a ***hope****."* (Jeremiah 29:11)

"The LORD is my portion," says my soul, "Therefore I have ***hope*** *in Him. . ."* (Lamentations 3:24)

"AND IN HIS NAME THE GENTILES WILL ***HOPE****."* (Matthew 12:21)

. . .and perseverance, proven character; and proven character, ***hope****; and* ***hope*** *does not disappoint, because the love of God has been poured out within our hearts through the Holy Spirit who was given to us.* (Romans 5:4-5)

*Find the translation that best suits you, and fill your heart with this living word.

The Secret of God

God, our God, will take care of ***the hidden things*** *but the revealed things are our business. It's up to us and our children to attend to all the terms in this Revelation.* Deuteronomy 29:29 (The Message)

The secret things *belong unto the Lord our God, but the things which are revealed belong to us and to our children forever, that we may do all of the words of this law.* – Deuteronomy 29:29 (Amplified)

At one time I believed that God randomly chose people (a select, elite few) to operate in the miraculous, giving them powerful, life-changing ministries. I no longer adhere to that belief. I now believe that God is preparing a mighty army to touch His world now, today! This army is a massive force, one that has been taught much and taught well. Make no mistake, we are well equipped – it is time we rise up and operate in that which we know.

The Lord our God has made Himself available, through His Holy Spirit, to empower us in our purpose. It is not His plan for us to float about aimlessly. He established order in His Kingdom from The Beginning – by default we live in a world lost to the rule of disorder. Our purpose is to regain that order. He has done all the preliminary work for us to take back all that has been lost. He did not do all this so we could just have church. He wants a loving, ongoing relationship with us, but more, He wants us to live in His miraculous realm so that we can affect the necessary change in this world. Some of you may not want to change the world at large, but you wouldn't mind changing the one around you – right? In the following pages, I will explore the power already available to you to accomplish your purpose.

SPIRIT-TO-*SPIRIT* CONNECTION
The Ultimate Download

Let us look at His universal, foundational principals – God's creative secret. The operational ability of this secret comes directly from His Spirit to our spirit. The power, which when received and applied, will allow us to be one of *those people* who is influential – a leader – a life-changer and one who regularly operates in the miraculous. These principals elevate us from mere "pew warmers" to lives flowing with "milk and honey." What does that mean? It means lives that are whole and healthy with ample supply to nurture, love and empower others – all in great abundance from the Spirit of God, your partner in this process.

These character qualities were deposited in us when we were created. They can only be understood and allowed to grow, however, by a Spirit-to-*spirit* connection. The grace of God is a supernatural power enabling us to do and be all that He has called us to be. Beloved, grace is not a "Get Out of Jail Free" card like the one in the game Monopoly. Grace doesn't give me permission to do that which is wrong. Grace does not protect me from the consequences of my choices. Grace gives me the power to do that which I cannot. This is good news. You only need to be willing, and He will do the work of establishing this powerful quality in you to function from and through you with natural ease. He is not going to force this on you. His Spirit and your *spirit* are connected. You must allow this connection to produce the physical, emotional and mental changes in you – it is as simple and as difficult as that.

Listed below are ten wonderful words, valuable to successful human relationships. And to one degree or another, we understand them and are all able to operate in them when we want to, but not purely and not consistently. The Spirit-to-*spirit* connection not only allows you to operate in them purely and consistently but POWERFULLY and eventually easily. They are:

Love
Unity
Forgiveness
Faith
Humility
Perspective
Gratitude and Generosity
Integrity and Honor

The Apostle Paul knew these wonderful qualities, walked in them, and exposed them in every letter he wrote. These are not just nice letters with good instruction; they are the Word of God, divinely inspired. Therefore, they are living, CREATIVE energy that propels us in our purpose – the provision for our purpose – the conduit (if you will) that pulls what we need (mentally, emotionally, physically, financially and spiritually) from the spirit realm into our physical realm.

This power is not hidden from His children. Unfortunately, I have had a semi-passive relationship with Him for twenty-plus years. I finally understand the necessity, origin, and power of the grace of God. It is necessary for success in any undertaking. In my passive state I didn't understand the importance of it nor did I appropriate it. This is not a statement of regret as much as it is a statement of fact. Most of us live in a passive existence. Even those of us with goals achieve them only to set another goal in an effort to establish significance against a standard of little importance. Or we set goals, fail to achieve them, and live in presumed failure. Our significance and our success are in Him. Connected to Him I am able to "*do all things through Christ...*" Phil. 4:13 (KJV)

Living life in this earthly realm disconnected from our mighty creator is a disabled existence – regardless of our wealth, power, success or accomplishments. We all have a purpose with eternal consequences. I just never dreamed I could be of any real use to the Kingdom of God, so I never pursued it – is that what you believe? I hope through this inspired word you might be persuaded otherwise.

I am not attempting to write a formula or a how-to book, but an accumulation of simple truth to enable us to live, really live, in **joy, liberty, wisdom and abundance. I want to live on purpose, with a purpose that leaves an indelible imprint on the little corner of the world I get to touch.** Please know this is not a religious book of what you need TO DO to be a Christian or what you need TO DO to walk in supernatural power. This is about relationship and what you can become when connected (Spirit-to-spirit) with your Father God.

Many of us complicate this simple truth or we box it up and put conditions on it which render it (and us) powerless. This simple truth is mighty on its own, but when you acknowledge grace as the power (intentionally and on purpose) then there is nothing impossible. This is HIS desire, beloved.

TO KNOW HIM

At this point, I will not assume you know Him, so we will look at how to begin that very important relationship. First, He is God, the only God. He is three in one: The Father, the Son and the Spirit. He is Holy – we are not. He came to our realm as the man Jesus. Jesus came to show us the Father's great love and to become the bridge connecting God (Holy) and us (unholy) rendering us holy.

Jesus became the perfect sacrifice to allow us the extraordinary opportunity to become a friend of God, but even more, His child. . .

> *See how great a love the Father has bestowed on us, that we would be called children of God; and such we are for this reason the world does not know us, because it did not know Him. Beloved, now we are*

> *children of God, and it has not appeared as yet what we will be; we know that when He appears, we will be like Him, because we will see Him just as He is.*
> I John 3:1-2 (NAS, emphasis mine). (See also John 14: 15-31)

Now, the Holy Spirit has been dispatched to finish the work of making us like Him (John 14).

How Do I Know?

In September 1980 this relationship opportunity was presented to me. I did not understand all the theology associated with it, and indeed, it seemed too simple to be true – almost too simple to accept. I was ready to reject it when the presenter made this statement, which I share with you today.

"Well, ask God," she said. "If He is real, and you are sincere, He will show Himself to you. If He is not, you are no worse off." How can you argue with that kind of logic? So, about noon on October 1, 1980, I did, and He did. I simply said, "God, I don't know if you are real, and I don't know if Jesus is really your Son, but I need to know, and I need to know now."

Beloved, His presence – both gentle and powerful - filled the room, and filled my heart with an acceptance I had never known. At that moment, I asked Him to take over my life and be my God. The love, acceptance, and hope that filled my heart are far beyond anything I had ever experienced. I knew something major had taken place, and indeed it had. He infused my spirit with His Life.

I have a friend who in 1973 lost his 8-year-old daughter to death. He soon fell into a very dark place – the grief overwhelming. For three years he tried his dead level best to come out of that dark place. He confessed to me that he tried Positive Thinking, it did not work; he tried covering himself in work – hoping to find purpose, it did not work; he almost killed himself with alcohol, still no relief. Then through a series of events and encounters, he was introduced to the Lord Jesus Christ and the darkness began to leave.

Today he has had a full personal and professional life and recently retired from the top position of his company. He and his wife have two more daughters and eight grandchildren. He is one of the strongest, most stable, peaceful, and loving people I know, the very image of Jesus Christ. He gives God all the glory and takes every opportunity to share God's mercy and love with the world around him.

I challenge you: if you aren't sure, give Him the same chance I gave Him – do it now. I am not asking you to become religious – far from it. I am offering you a free pass to real life.

PRAYER

Do you have an active, personal relationship with God through Jesus Christ? If you do not, this is where you start. Pray this with me:

> *God, I don't know for sure if you are real, but I need You to hear me. I don't know if Jesus is real and I don't understand this apart from the religion I have been taught. But if you are real and you can hear me I need to know it and I need to know it now.*

If you were sincere in praying this prayer, then He has made Himself known to you by now. So, you need to take the next step. Say,

> *I give you my life, I receive Your Life, and ask that You come in, save and heal me. Forgive me of my sins and help me live the life you have for me.*

The next step is equally important: tell someone. Be sure it is someone you can trust, someone who will build and encourage you. Naturally, try to find someone who will be happy for you and validate your choice. Many will rejoice with you, unfortunately not all.

UNDERSTANDING SPIRIT-TO-*SPIRIT*

Nicodemus did not understand this concept when he discussed it with Jesus in the gospel of John (chapter 3), and frankly, neither did I until I experienced it. Becoming a child of God is not something you join; it is something you are born into – a relational process. You ask Jesus to come into your life and God's Spirit then gives life to your spirit. Presto! Your Spirit is now alive to God, connected to the Spirit of God – the Creator of the universe and everything in it.

> *But as many as received Him, to them He gave the right to become children of God, even to those who believe in His name, who were born, not of blood nor of the will of the flesh nor of the will of man, but of God.* John 1:12-13 (NAS)

We come into relationship with Jesus by acknowledging our condition, accepting His forgiveness and receiving the surge of life into our spirit by His Holy Spirit. Prior to this, our lives have been directed by our intellect, our emotions and our physical desires – in short, from our soul and body. Our soul is basically who we are – our mind, our personality and our emotions. This change connects the life of God to our spirit, it brings us into the family of God and transfers us, in the Spirit realm, from the kingdom of this world to the **Kingdom of God.**

There is a vast, unseen world around us called the spirit realm, The Kingdom of God and the kingdom of this world are both all around us, yet not all are visible. Without going into great detail let me simply say when you become a Christian, you are marked in such a way that all who occupy the spirit realm know who you are and to whom you are related.

God does not patch up the old life, or make certain repairs on the old life; He gives a new life, through the new birth.

Kathryn Kuhlman

I am a firm believer that no one reaches adulthood without some degree of wounding in our soul and bodies. Much of the physical wounds heal by adulthood, but the soul – emotional wounds – are another issue all together. We learn all kinds of survival techniques, but there is a vast difference in survival and freedom. Only the healing power of God, flowing through our newly alive spirit, can bring complete healing and wholeness to our wounded souls. He will certainly heal, given the opportunity.

As we come into this new, living relationship with the Lord Jesus, everything around us still looks the same. Our circumstances have not changed, but trust me, YOU have moved. Your identity is changing, you have new spiritual DNA, and you really are becoming a new person. It does not matter how you feel; it doesn't matter that you cannot figure it out; what has begun, has begun. In viewing the Word of God how you feel and what you think are not prerequisites to this change. (John 5:24)

Therefore if anyone is in Christ, he is a new creature; the old things passed away; behold, new things have come. II Corinthians 2:15 (NAS)

Furthermore, this new location, of which Christ is the center and the life-giver, has been opened up to us. The features of this new world are completely foreign to our thoughts and altogether beyond our intellectual understanding – and can be known only by divine revelation. I have come to realize that I operated out of my intelligence and my emotions (my soul) most of the time. Even after becoming a Christian I have lived out of my soul; mostly, because it was what I had always known, because I thought change was up to me. I did not know God's Spirit could change and heal my soul through my spirit – like a clean, virus-free download from His Spirit to mine.

Most of us in the twenty-first century understand that our computers have software that causes them to function. If this software has been damaged by use or viruses, it becomes dysfunctional. Naturally, you can uninstall and reinstall the software, but that is time consuming and does not guarantee that it will repair the problem. Often a software patch is required from the developer. Ultimately, the act of providing patches to projects ensures that an organization has a cheaper upgrade path and at the same time they help to ensure that the software they depend on remains in active development. It's a win-win.

It is the same concept with our reconnection to God. Our life, with our spirit disconnected from our creator, makes our whole being (mind, body and spirit) dysfunctional. To be truly functional in this life we must reconnect our spirit to God's Spirit and submit our soul (mind, will and emotions) and our body to the leadership of our spirit. At first this process is difficult because we have adapted to and are comfortable with our mind, our will, our emotions and our body dictating our every step. However, by our determined choice this transference of power is accomplished. Life in the Spirit becomes almost as natural as breathing.

Salvation is FREE, the benefits of salvation (a whole and functional life) require obedient determination. Obedience is simply our willingness to submit to His tender, loving, and merciful heart so He can do the work in and through us. I am not saying that our intelligence and our emotions are terrible or wrong. I submit the contrary, they are wonderful – God created them and gave them to us. My soul needs to be healed and surrendered to my Spirit, as it is connected to His for me to function at my highest and my best. Without this order it is a disabled existence. Quite frankly, it is a religious existence. You know the religious life, don't you? It is made up of strict rules and boundaries; high standards that can't be met. Religion is bondage and death. Jesus said He came to set us free (Romans 8:2).

THERE ARE THREE KINDS OF PEOPLE

We humans are predominately stationed in one of these three positions with the ability to progressively move from one state to another. I list these positions for reference only. Where you are positioned is a personal choice. As I said earlier, God has made Himself available through His Spirit for us to become all we are destined to be.

1. **The Natural Person:** This is a person who is not a Christian (not in relationship with God through Jesus Christ). He is led by the natural self, ruled by his physical, emotional and mental appetites – what is good and feels the best for him is what he does. He may even belong to and attend a church or another religious organization. Even the most moral, intelligent and good person is still dysfunctional in this state. Few, however, are moral and good.

   > *But the natural man receiveth not the things of the Spirit of God: for they are foolishness unto him: neither can he know them, because they are Spiritually discerned.* Corinthians 2:14 (KJV)

2. **The Soul (or carnal) Person:** The word carnal is a word that is not used much these days except in religious settings or artsy movies. However, it relates to somebody's physical needs or appetites, especially as contrasted with spiritual qualities. Simply put, a carnal person is predominately led by the soul. This is a person who is truly a born again Christian, but never allows his spirit to grow and, therefore, never really functions in his true spiritual destiny (a perpetual spiritual infant). This person probably goes to church and may know the Bible

intellectually, but does not know or understand it with his spirit; there is a difference.

> *And I, brethren, could not speak to you as to spiritual men, but as to men of flesh, as to infants in Christ. I gave you milk to drink, not solid food; for you were not yet able to receive it. Indeed, even now you are not yet able, for you are still fleshly. For since there is jealousy and strife among you, are you not fleshly, and are you not walking like mere men?*
> I Corinthians 4:1-4 (KJV)

3. **The Spiritual Person:** This is the person led by the Spirit of God, with a Spirit to *spirit* connection. One who is born again, seeking after God for a relationship that will transform him and his world. He knows the Word of God, but, ***more***, he asks the Spirit of God to give his spirit true understanding.

This is where the story of the caterpillar and the butterfly is best understood. The caterpillar is just a worm, living and getting by on vegetation near the ground. Then something from within starts to stir and the little worm, **<u>through a process to which he can only surrender,</u>** begins to be transformed literally from the inside out into the most beautiful of creatures. This new creation goes from living on vegetation to flying from bloom to bloom, living on sweet nectar and pollinating as he goes (changing his world).

> *Now we have received, not the spirit of the world, but the Spirit who is from God, so that we may know the things freely given to us by God,* I Corinthians 2:12 (KJV)

SPIRIT, SOUL AND BODY

Coming to God, becoming a Christian as I did, restored the missing ingredient to wholeness – a Living Spirit – connected to God. I now have the elements needed to live a life of wholeness and victory. However, for the longest time my mind and my emotions, which had always ruled my life, wanted to continue to rule my life. The real work of change comes from my connection with God and **the submission of my soul to the process**. Beloved, it IS a process.

Have you ever been to the performance of a symphony orchestra? There are many different and wonderful instruments played by gifted artists. Always prior to a performance there is a time where the musicians come on stage to tune their instruments, making them ready for the performance. I am sure, at this point, if pressed, they could perform together reasonably well. To play at their best, two important and necessary ingredients must be added: the first violin and the conductor.

We humans are wonderful and gifted, but we need the connection to God to perform at our best. The First Violin is our Living Spirit. We received life into our spirit when we invite Him to live in us. Composers often assign the melody to the first violin, while second violins play harmony, accompaniment patterns or the melody an octave lower than the first violin. The conductor (composer) is the Spirit of God. All instruments must be played as directed by the conductor; otherwise, it is not music.

Your life before becoming a Christian is a life without a First Violin (no melody) and without a Conductor (no order). So turning things around will be a process. My Spirit is willing. My soul doesn't want to play second violin, but God has a plan. He has written a symphony for us – we are the symphony. He wants us to partner with Him to accomplish this plan – to play this beautiful music. We are His magnificent song. We must allow the Secret to be woven into the fabric of who we are in order to impact our world, just as the Apostle

Paul did and countless others who have chosen to apply the Secret – this beautiful music to their lives.

Music of The Heart

Do you know that our hearts make music that we cannot hear? Yes, it's true! When we seek to worship our Savior, with our motive focused on blessing Him and Him alone, our hearts make music that only He can hear. When a group of believers get together and enter into genuine, pure-hearted worship, the music our hearts make becomes a beautiful harmony to His heart. Yes, we all have a different and distinct heart song, and when combined becomes an indescribable, delightful harmony to His ears.

Things that mute the music of our heart are selfish ambition, anger, unforgiveness, and pride. These dishonor the Spirit and distort the connection between His Spirit and mine. People may appear to us to be bright and shiny as a new penny and absorbed in worship, but the word of God says man looks at the outward appearance, but the LORD looks at the heart.

Those of us taught to type from the home position of the keyboard are aware that if we position our hands just one key off, that which we type is not understandable. If we start to worship and are just one key off, the melody of our heart is not a pleasure to hear. Worship from the heart causes the Spirit of God to manifest in beautiful and powerful expressions, meeting our needs without ever asking. Enjoy His benefits (presence) today by making melody with your heart to the Lord.

> . . .speaking to one another in psalms and hymns and spiritual songs, singing and making melody *with your heart* to the Lord . . . (Ephesians 5:19)

> *What is the outcome then? I will pray with the spirit and I will pray with the mind also; I will sing with the*

spirit and I will sing with the mind also. (I Corinthians 14:15)

But the LORD said to Samuel, "Do not consider his appearance or his height, for I have rejected him. The LORD does not look at the things man looks at. Man looks at the outward appearance, but the LORD looks at the heart." I Samuel 16:7

All (NAS)

Watch Your Mouth

The Secret to Love, Forgiveness, and Unity

> *Use your heads as you live and work among outsiders. Don't miss a trick. Make the most of every opportunity. Be gracious in your speech. The goal is to bring out the best in others in conversation, not put them down, and not cut them out.* Colossians 4:6 (The Message)

We want pleasant things drawn to us, not dreadful, correct? We want people drawn to us, not repelled, correct? Grumpy, cold, indifferent and coarse people will draw that type of energy into their lives. Yes, we can be misunderstood, but we can correct that. There will be many who we will not be able to touch. However, they will not soon forget us when we intentionally operate in the Secret of God because there is warmth associated with us of which we are not aware.

> *The mouth of a righteous man is a well of life.* (Proverbs 10:11)

> *...the tongue of the wise is health.* (Prov. 12:18)

> *He that keepeth his mouth keepeth his life; but he that openeth wide his lips shall have destruction.* (Proverbs 13:3)

> *A man's belly is satisfied with the fruit of his mouth and with the increase of his lips shall he be filled;*

Death and life are in the power of the tongue*; and they that love it shall eat the fruit thereof.* (Proverbs 18:20, 21)

(all KJV)

A spiritual law that few recognize is that our confession rules us. It is what we confess with our lips that really dominates our inner being.

– F. F. Bosworth

It is written: *"I believed; therefore I have spoken."* Psalm 116:10 and *"With that same spirit of faith we also believe and therefore speak,"* II Corinthians 4:13 (KJV). According to the Bible in Genesis, EVERYTHING we see was created when God SPOKE. Genesis also states that we are made in His image and His likeness. Both of these concepts by themselves are powerful. Many people know the power of the words they speak and use that power to form their world. They use this power and the authority they have assumed to control people. Parents and teachers build or destroy the children assigned to them with their words. Employers create the atmosphere and morale among their staff with their words. Remember, too, a diagnosis or a promise are simply words. I believe you can take a diagnosis, a broken promise, or hurtful words to God. He has the final word on any subject. It is His great pleasure to take the facts of your experience and trade them for His truth.

I am not promoting a "name it and claim it" mentality. I am simply stating the origin of the power of words. As children of the Most High God, what we say, what comes out of our mouth has a creative quality blessing and cursing, so "Watch Your Mouth!"

3 *Then God said, "Let there be light"; and there was light. . .*

11 *Then God said, "Let the earth sprout vegetation, plants yielding seed, and fruit trees on the*

> *earth bearing fruit after their kind with seed in them"; **and it was so**.* Genesis 1:3 and 11 (NIV)

> *Set a **watch**, O LORD, before my **mouth**; keep the door of my lips.* Psalm 141:3 (KJV)

THE SECRET OF LOVE

The love of God produces love. Genetically, it cannot produce anything else. Love is not an emotion, but true emotion flows from it. The Love of God is a LIVING thing; a living thing that He can plant in you. This is NOT something you can do; this is something you have to choose to ask God to do in you. In ourselves (flesh/soul) there is NO Godly love. He has to grow it there; we must intentionally allow it.

Saint John wrote, "God is love". I take that literally – He doesn't have love, **<u>He is love</u>**! In Paul's letter to the Galatians (5:1-6) he reminded them that: *"It was for freedom that Christ set us free; therefore keep standing firm and do not be subject again to a yoke of slavery."*

> *Behold I, Paul, say to you that if you receive circumcision, Christ will be of no benefit to you. And I testify again to every man who receives circumcision that he is under obligation to keep the whole Law. You have been severed from Christ, you who are seeking to be justified by law; <u>you have fallen from grace</u>. For we through the Spirit, by faith, are waiting for the hope of righteousness. For in Christ Jesus neither circumcision nor uncircumcision means anything, **<u>but faith working through love.</u>*** (NAS, emphasis mine)

Basically, Paul is saying, If you think you can do it yourself, you are deluded. No one ever has and no one ever will. The law was given to show us what is expected. It shows me how desperately I need Him. I need the power of His grace to enable my faith to work through love. His grace produces His love in me.

I remember the first time I heard the Greek word *Agape*, which literally means "the love God has toward you," my perspective of I Corinthians, chapter 13 was changed forever. Paul begins the chapter by saying (and I paraphrase), *"If I know all the power of God, but if I don't understand His love for me and thereby allow that love to operate in me in this world, what value is my understanding and His power? I am just using energy and making noise, no one is transformed. I am just marking time and getting stuff."*

Read the balance of that chapter, as Paul wrote it, understanding and receiving the Love (*Agape*) God has for us, and then allow the power of the grace of God to genetically reproduce in your spirit His love for you and His love for others. You do this by choice. You simply say, "Father, I do not know Your love for me; please place it in me; help me to experience it. I do not have the ability to love others, but I am willing to let your love so fill me that it flows to others. And, Father, I do not know how to love you as I should; please place that in me, too." AMEN.

Pray this often. The transformation will begin within you – from His Spirit to your spirit then outward.

- The Love (of God toward me) is patient,
- The Love (of God toward me) is kind,
- The Love (of God toward me) does not envy,
- The Love (of God toward me) does not boast,
- The Love (of God toward me) is not proud,
- The Love (of God toward me) is not rude,
- The Love (of God toward me) is not self-seeking,
- The Love (of God toward me) is not easily angered,
- The Love (of God toward me) keeps no record of wrongs,
- The Love (of God toward me) does not delight in evil but rejoices with the truth,
- The Love (of God toward me) always protects, always trusts, always hopes, and always perseveres.

- The Love (of God toward me) never fails. . .And now these three remain: faith, hope and love. But the greatest of these is LOVE. I Corinthians 13 (NIV) (emphasis mine)

This is what is expected of us – not optional – but we cannot produce this on our own. It requires our connection to the Holy Spirit and our willingness to allow Him to produce it in us.

Saint John referred to himself (several times) in the Gospel he wrote as “the disciple whom Jesus loved.” I believe that before any of his brother disciples, he understood and knew Jesus was God and he knew and understood God’s love toward him. John was the ONLY male disciple to go and stay at the cross while Jesus died there for him. He was also the first to believe Jesus had risen from the dead, and one of the first to see Him alive after His resurrection. Naturally, I cannot say this for sure, but it wouldn’t surprise me if this is where Paul received his understanding of God’s love and thereby wrote, what I call, the Love Chapter.

There will come a time, if you are not already there, that you will know the Love God has for you, and with that transforming knowledge are able to allow the expression of His Love to flow to the world around you. Paul instructs us in his letter to the Ephesians (6th chapter) by saying,

> *. . .having girded your loins with truth, and having put on the breastplate of righteousness, and having shod your feet with the preparation of the gospel of peace; withal taking up the shield of faith, wherewith ye shall be able to quench all the fiery darts of the evil (one). And take the helmet of salvation, and the sword of the Spirit, which is the word of God.* (ASV).

This armor is spirit armor, because our battle is not against flesh and blood people, it is a spirit battle (II Cor. 10: 3-5). These weapons and armor are mighty and necessary, make no mistake about it. It is important that we do a mind shift at this point and remember that the people coming against us need the love of God flowing toward them. Our battle is with the evil force that is behind and driving these people. We all know that getting dressed requires first a layer of undergarments. Therefore, before you put on your armor, you should put on the undergarment of LOVE. The greatest protection you will ever have is the layer of love between your body and your armor. Everything we do must flow from the love of God. . .even warfare.

About the time I came to know the Lord, I had a broken and contentious relationship with a family member. This was very difficult in that often we were required to be together. I loved her and I hated her. This broken relationship was one of the catalysts that propelled me into my relationship with God. It seemed no matter what I did or didn't do, it was always wrong. I wanted this friendship repaired, but I was unable to repair it even with my best efforts. So I tried something radical; I asked God to love her through me. I promised to keep my mouth shut and say only what He wanted me to say, which was precious little. I wasn't always successful at this, but I was always quick to apologize first to her and then to God. I freely admit, it was easier to apologize to God than to her.

Ever so slightly, things began to change, week upon week. Within a year, no one would have guessed that we had ever had a problem. Several years later she asked me how I could have loved her back then. I replied, "What do you mean?" And she said, "Every time I was around you, I could feel your love for me." That was the powerful love of God she felt. He was gracious to me and answered my radical prayer. This experience also began to teach me the vast difference in my ability to love and His love in me.

DAILY DIETARY SUPPLEMENT: L.O.J.
(Love of Jesus)

Dosage: (Recommended Daily Allowance) Take at least one daily – more, if necessary. Long term use will cause it to reproduce within you.

Developed to annihilate the following harmful viral agents: jealousy, covetousness, resentment, distrust, boastfulness, arrogance, conceit, pride, self-importance, rudeness, offensiveness, disrespect, selfishness, demanding, egotism, irritability, bad temper, petulance, personal offense.

Active *supernatural* ingredients: PATIENCE, KINDNESS

Long term use causes you to:

1. Become tenacious, never giving up on yourself or others
2. Believe the best of yourself and others
3. Be hopeful always
4. Endure through every circumstance
5. Love beyond the offense

Pharmaceutical name: Agape
L.O.J. (Love of Jesus) Never Fails

For testimonials on the effectiveness of this product, visit this web site: www.bible.com and search for: John, Peter, Paul, James, Timothy, Titus, Matthew, Mark, Luke, Jesus.

THE SECRET OF FORGIVENESS

We have been forgiven much, therefore much (and often) forgiveness is required of us. Being forgiven and giving forgiveness are a CHOICE we have to make. Forgiving is not optional if we want to stay in relationship with our Lord (Matt. 6:15). Receiving and giving are two sides of the same coin. Receiving is oftentimes easier than giving. Both, however, require power from the Spirit to spirit connection to truly be accomplished. Forgiving is difficult with a broken heart. Even time cannot heal that. Only God can do the healing work in you so you can receive the seed of forgiveness. Like all good seed in good ground, it will produce. Trust me, beloved, it had to be this simple for me to get it. He is faithful and just (true to His own nature and promises) to forgive me when I ask sincerely. No, I don't deserve it, can't do anything to pay for it, and can't appease Him to keep it. Because it is settled, He will not take it back. He will not stop forgiving me, as long as I ask.

> *If we [freely] admit that we have sinned and confess our sins, He is faithful and just (true to His own nature and promises) and will forgive our sins [dismiss our lawlessness] and [continuously] cleanse us from all unrighteousness [every-thing not in conformity to His will in purpose, thought, and action]."* I John 1:9 (Amplified)

Now, how do I turn that coin over? I am not divine. I do not have within me supernatural abilities to forgive and love, right? Wrong! Basically, within us (our human soul) is no good thing, but remember, The Spirit of God is connected to our spirit now and His grace flows between us to empower us in this process. This fact certainly gives us the ability, but it doesn't make it easy. We must contend for it!

A friend and I were talking recently about a situation she was involved in that resulted in the loss of her job. She needed desperately to forgive these people and to be free of the bondage to them through unforgiveness. She was consumed with daily obsessions about the injustices of the people and the events of this situation. It was making her physically sick and it was almost all she could talk about. She lived in this state for almost two years. On one occasion she said, "I want to forgive, but it is such a challenge." I agreed with her that when we are doing it ourselves it is impossible. Forgiveness is a work of the Spirit in our spirit, not a mental or emotional work. If we wait until our mind and our emotions want to forgive, we have quite a long wait. I told her what I tell myself, "You must CHOOSE to let God do the work in you. It is a process."

There may be many roads to forgiving – they all must cross through the Spirit of God, however, to be real and lasting. This is a story of the way I learned how to allow Him to do this wonderful work in me:

Several years ago a young man began a work of cold, calculated, intentional harm and injury against my daughter and her two children. To go into detail about all that was done would fill more pages than three other books this size. I allowed that person's actions to fill my heart with anger toward him. Anger, given enough food and time, turns into hate – the kind of hate that says, "I hope he dies a long and painful death, a death I get to watch, and he burns in hell forever." This kind of hate carries with it many mental fantasies.

Our body reacts to fantasy the same as it reacts to reality. Correspondingly, the Spirit of God is grieved by this kind of hate. This hate was my companion for well over two years. I knew it was wrong, but I felt powerless to change how I felt. I knew I needed to forgive, but try as I might, hate was the only emotion I had. God is good, gracious, and merciful, and He contended with me. According to the Bible, He knows my heart. I didn't have to tell Him my hate was wrong. I was becoming bitter and obsessed with vengeful fantasies. I was powerless to change my heart to feel differently – He knew that before I admitted it.

So, you know what I did; I made a CHOICE to forgive. Each time my mind played one of the past events or a new event happened, I trained myself to stop the thought process and say (out loud), "I forgive!" I had to do this over and over and over again. Eventually, I was even able to say, "Bless him." Often the words, bless him, caught in my throat. This went on for several months, sometimes daily, sometimes hourly – two steps forward and one step back or one step forward and two steps back, but I didn't give in to giving up.

I eventually learned to stop the memory of each event before it played out in full. Each time something new would happen, I would have to go back to square one and start the process again. Each time I asked God to forgive me and help me make the choice. My emotions never changed, but in the face of each negative emotion, I said (out loud), "I forgive. Please Lord, bless him." I graduated to an even higher place (still, I felt hate) and was able to choose to say, "Lord, I know you love him. Help me to love him."

One Saturday afternoon a friend called and asked me if I would tape a ballgame on TV for him. I went to the cabinet and dug out several old videotapes to find one I could use to tape my friend's program. The first two were labeled, so I set them aside. I popped the third in the VCR and found it to be my grandson Jordan's first birthday party, which I thought I had lost. One of the first people I saw on the tape was my Mom, who had passed away some four years previously. I forgot about my friend's recording and sat down to re-enjoy this event.

Shortly into the recording, in the background, I heard his voice, the one I hated. I forgot he had been at that party. I was almost sure it was him, but I couldn't see him. The camera kept moving through the assembled group, but did not land on him. Finally, and it seemed an eternity, there he was! I hit the pause button; I was sitting on the very edge of my couch; my heart was pounding in my chest, I could hardly breathe…there he was, in the room with me…and…I did not hate him. The love of God filled my body and flowed through time to him. It was finished; it was done. Forgiveness had replaced the hate in my heart, and I hadn't even realized it until I was face-to-face with him. You see, I believed God and He credited it to me as forgiveness. I couldn't do it, but I chose to believe He could…and He did.

This has been tested many times, my friend, and I am still in forgiveness. I still love, and he is still trying to hurt the people I love. But, beloved, it isn't him; it is the enemy of God using him. This doesn't mean that God is alright with this person hurting my daughter. He is not, and He is taking care of this, His way. I am also learning that I have the authority to speak to and bind those harassing spirits, which I do. My authority is enhanced (super multiplied) by the fact that I am operating in the love of God. I have learned so very much through this situation.

Do you know what I do each and every time something happens? I forgive, ask for God's blessings on this young man, and stand up in the authority I have been given against the enemy. I command him (the enemy) to stop, I command him to be quiet, I invoke the name of Jesus and the enemy must obey! God is a good and just God. He will not stand by and allow this to continue forever. He has made me a promise: *the people I love will be set free from this tyranny.* Along with Moses I say, "Let my people go!" (Ex. 5:1) God will do this, because He promised and I believe.

THE SECRET OF UNITY

Unity produces more than peace from disagreements; it multiplies the power of prayer and spiritual warfare.

> *And ye shall chase your enemies, and they shall fall before you by the sword. And five of you shall chase an hundred, and an hundred of you shall put ten thousand to flight: and your enemies shall fall before you by the sword.* Leviticus 26:7-8 (KJV)

This sounds like super-multiplied power – that is the product of UNITY. Unity is not about getting along with our fellow Christians, it is about being in agreement with God. If the only thing we Christians can agree on is <u>Jesus is Lord</u> – that is enough. If I am busy proving my point or persuading others to believe as I do, I am wasting precious time and strength. Agreement with God is not about doctrine or dogma, it is about being in agreement with His Word and with His Spirit. Being in unity with God means finding the truth in His word, agreeing with it, and asking Him to accomplish it in and through us. Being obedient to the truth of His word requires His help, from His Spirit to our spirit – we must choose to allow this. Am I sounding like a broken record? Repetition is an excellent teacher.

> *"Again I say unto you, That if* ***two*** *of you shall agree on earth as* ***touching*** *anything that they shall ask, it*

> *shall be done for them of my Father which is in heaven."* Matthew 18:19 (KJV)

Yes, unity produces a pleasant life when we walk in it with friends and family (Psalms 133:1). That is important and cannot be done without the power of my unity with Him. Without my connection to Him, I can only have peace with friends and family by being a door mat. Door mats are passive. Christians united with Christ are warriors. To be united with Christ transforms us into Kingdom People.

What are Kingdom People? For this I will quote Dutch Sheets from a presentation given in January, 2008:

> *The Kingdom is the domain of God, His rule in any situation (any place, anywhere). So if we mention the church in any context outside the Kingdom, we're going to get in trouble. Eclaceia – a governmental or legislative term* (Eclaceia: a Greek word translated in the Bible as Church). *A group of people the King is going to rule through on the earth. Until you think like a governing body you are not functioning like the church He was talking about and intends to build. We must move from congregational thinking to congressional thinking. Authority flows out from the Kingdom, not from the church. Authority comes from the King. . . He is calling us to infect the earth with His Spirit. . .Kingdom disciples have eternity in their hearts and weapons in their hands. Kingdom thinkers are difference makers and culture shapers.*

- *Kingdom people ask God what He wants them to be. They live for eternal purposes not temporal.*
- *Kingdom people know that their gifts are from Him and for Kingdom purposes. They know that their destiny is what He planned for them not what they want.*

- *Kingdom people do not exist to make money – they exist to extend God's Kingdom into their world – money is a tool, not a goal. They are not millionaires; they are millionaire makers and million dollar givers. They live like caretakers and not owners of all they have.*
- *Kingdom people are not just healed; they are healers. They are not just saved people, they are people that save. They are creators not just consumers. They feed; they don't just eat.*
- *Kingdom people know they are part of the solution so they would rather work than whine. They know it's not about them, so they don't complain, they just do it. They are committed to a cause; they are not just sheep looking for greener pastures. They know that they are His partner and not His hireling. They become God's answer, not His problem.*
- *Kingdom people are heavenly minded, not earthly. They do not judge by the carnal mindset of the world when it comes to greatness, success or morality.*
- *Kingdom people understand the realm of the Spirit. I think we are going to move into a place where we understand the realm of the spirit in a completely higher level than we have ever moved in before. We are going to realize we are of a Kingdom that is not earth bound.*
- *Kingdom people live by the word of God, not by what they think or feel or what they were taught by contradicting forces.*
- *Kingdom people pray. They believe in the supernatural. They believe in miracles – the supernatural is not a stretch for them – they are*

supernatural themselves. They believe God owns everything and can do anything. Because of this, they are dangerous; they are boat rockers, and they turn their world right-side-up. They know God; they have seen him. Therefore, they hate mediocrity, average, run-of-the-mill, compromise, lethargy and the status quo. That's why they hate religiosity that standardizes mediocrity.

- *Kingdom people. . .believe in things they cannot see; they see a future that does not as yet exist and they create it. . .*
- *Kingdom people love to worship not just sing. They know they can connect and commune with God. Therefore, religious routine is boring and senseless to them. They insist in knowing and relating to God not to a system, a custom or another person.*
- *Kingdom people don't (just) go to church, they are the church.*

When we expand our thinking to a Kingdom world view everything is going to change because every situation we step into we are going to realize that we are there to extend the dominion of God in that place. We are going to begin to live in the Lord's prayer... Thy Kingdom come, Thy will be done on earth as it is in heaven..., we aren't going to be earthbound any longer in our thinking – we are going to move into a realm of revelation that moves us far above anything we have known before. We are going to be dangerous Kingdom people wherever we go. . .

This may sound radical to some, but to be in unity with our Lord actually causes the precious Holy Spirit to flow into and through us without effort.

> *. . . I in them and you in me. May they be brought to complete unity to let the world know that you sent me and have loved them even as you have loved me.* John 17:23 (NIV)

To be in unity is to have the same purpose, the same mind-set, the same faith and expectation, the same hope, the same vision as the Lord. It is also to be in agreement with what God says about you. Unity is a choice – a Spirit choice. The Secret of God is the tool for HIS purposes!

We all have different jobs, different paths and different gifts – with one Lord. We can see in the Bible that Peter, John and Paul were men of very different personalities, set out onto very different mission fields, doing their work in very different ways – but they changed the world and maintained the whole focus of their work to establishing God's Kingdom. They were in unity with the Lord and **His Purpose.**

What does all this have to do with watching my mouth, you might ask?

> *A good man out of the good treasure of his heart bringeth forth that which is good; and an evil man out of the evil treasure of his heart bringeth forth that which is evil: for of the* ***abundance of the heart his MOUTH speaketh.*** Luke 6:45 (KJV, emphasis mine)

This scripture tells me that my mouth is connected to my heart. A heart, healed and connected to God, produces life in me and everyone I come into contact with – it brings forth that which is GOOD! The Secret of God is a good treasure in my heart. It is placed there by the Spirit-to-spirit connection. Only God can change a heart.

Something Out Of Nothing

The Secret of Faith

(Positive Expectation)

Romans 4:17 *Speaking of Abraham, Paul said. . .it is written: "I have made you a father of many nations." He is our father in the sight of God, in whom he believed—the God who gives life to the dead* ***and calls things that are not as though they were.*** (NIV)

Abraham believed God and it was ***credited*** *to him as righteousness.* Romans 4:3 (NIV)

Abraham received righteousness on credit (a certificate of debt). Righteousness is required to receive from God. Jesus had not yet paid the price on the cross, transferring righteousness and the extraordinary opportunity to receive freely all that God has, so God gave it to Abraham, on account, on credit. He was given a credit line to own his promise. What Abraham received by credit, we now have – Paid In Full.

. . .having canceled out the ***certificate of debt*** *consisting of decrees against us, which was hostile to us; and He has taken it out of the way, having nailed it to the cross.* Colossians 2:14 (NAS)

Our western mindset says, "I cannot believe it until I understand it. I need a plan that I can control". From this position my obedience is predicated by my being able to understand and see the end from the beginning. This mindset requires rules, intellectual order, analytical understanding and the pre-determined end.

Faith says, "Lord, I hear, I choose to believe, I choose to obey and the understanding will come. I do not understand why you require this and I don't have the ability to do it, but I'm willing to with your help. Help me trust You through this process."

> *Jesus said, "But* ***seek*** *ye first the kingdom of God, and* ***His righteousness****; and all these things shall be added unto you."* Matthew 6:33 (KJV) emphasis mine

The operative word in this passage is **SEEK**. This is not passive, it is an active pursuit of a loving relationship with him.

HIS RIGHTEOUSNESS – we don't have any, we can't produce any, it is His and it is established in us as we open up our spirit and spend time with Him (seek).

When we become Christians (become related to Him) we move into the Kingdom of God, but remain on earth. This Kingdom is unseen by the natural eye, it is, however, more real than what we see around us. Because, beloved, ***everything*** was created from this unseen realm. Everything we need comes from this realm.

> *So we fix our eyes not on what is seen, but on what is unseen. For what is seen is temporary, but what is unseen is eternal.* II Corinthians 4:18 (NAS)

> *. . . giving thanks to the Father,* ***who has qualified you*** *to share in the inheritance of the saints in the kingdom of light. For he has rescued us from the dominion of darkness and brought us into the kingdom of the Son he loves, in whom we have redemption, the forgiveness of sins.* (righteousness) Colossians 1:12-13 (NIV) (emphasis mine)

Righteous, His qualification, is not something we do like a religious act. It is something we become because of something He did, He does and He will do. It is simply something He puts on us, like clothing or a robe. Righteousness is something He must do for us. Righteousness, in simple terms, is right standing with God; to stand before Him with boldness and in confidence.

Abraham, who long before the work on the cross was accomplished, simply BELIEVED God. Twice Jesus said, "Only believe." (Mark 5:36; Luke 8:50). Believing is not a passive position; it is active position involving reading the Word of God, praying for understanding and expecting the power of God to enable me to be all He created me to be.

In the United States judicial system when we commit a crime, a file of charges is created with our name on it. These charges or this file is called our "Jacket". These charges must go before the judge; he is the final word on the law. At this point we must choose our defense.

We can defend ourselves or we can choose Jesus, our true advocate. If you choose to defend yourself, I've heard it said, "You have a fool for an attorney". Many defend themselves because they depend on their religion. We think our sin was somehow justified or that our sin is not as bad compared to others (could this be **PRIDE?**). Most of us, unfortunately, don't want to choose Jesus for any number of reasons.

The Prosecutor (the accuser of the brethren, Revelation 12:10) knows we deserve the full force and punishment of the law and he wants us to receive it.

However, if we swallow our pride and ask Jesus to be our defense attorney, here is what He does for us. He takes you before the judge, he then exchanges your "Jacket" for His and now the judge (the law) must release you because your jacket is now righteous. Jesus put on our filthy jacket and received our punishment.

In the story of the prodigal son (Luke 15), the father looked down the road, saw his son coming home and ran out to meet him. One of the things the father did was put his robe on his son. The son did nothing to deserve this. This robe was a symbol of their relationship – this symbolic act spoke volumes to everyone about his position in relation to the father. The son did nothing but come home. He made no religious promises.

> *But He was wounded for our transgressions, He was bruised for our iniquities; the chastisement of our peace was upon him; and with His stripes we are healed.* Isaiah 53:5 (KJV)

> *I greatly rejoice in the Lord, my soul shall be joyful in my God; for He hath covered me with the robe of righteousness. . .* Isaiah 61:10

Our righteousness comes from our relationship to God through Christ Jesus. This righteousness gives us access to the promises God has for us.

God has promises and plans and a purpose for you! You receive these by spending time in His Word and with Him. Write them down, pray over them and in the face of circumstances to the contrary, open your mouth and speak His Word on the subject, in faith, with expectation. That is exactly what Jesus did and He did it often (see Matthew 4).

Our mind asks, "HOW?!" I have a friend who calls it the "YBH" disorder: "Yes, But How?!"

We are not responsible for the HOW; God is responsible for the HOW. When your thoughts turn to trying to figure out HOW, remind yourself that your only responsibility is to trust and expect, then view it as done.

> *"God rejoices when we manifest a faith that holds Him to His Word."* Smith Wigglesworth

We need to recognize that we have many incorrect and distorted mindsets. These mindsets are contrary to the Spirit ruled mind. These mindsets need to be changed to agree in unity with our new living Spirit; we must deliberately render our thoughts subject to the Word of God.

> *And be not conformed to this world; but be ye transformed by the renewing of your mind. . .* Romans 12:2 (KJV)

Our thought processes have been established by life experiences, education, and people of significance, church, the media and so much more. An un-renewed mind is not a good judge of daily situations. The Word of God, which is THE truth, has quite a lot of competition in the realm of our mind.

That is why we must:

1. Hold up and **reconcile** our beliefs to the Word of God. Renounce all prejudice that is not backed up by the truth of God.
2. Use great wisdom in our choice of what we take into our minds until our Spirit mind is established.
3. Feed on the Truth.
4. Take all unbelief to Jesus and exchange it for Faith.

Expectation is the breeding ground of the promises and purposes of God. This expectation works both for the positive and for the negative; therefore we MUST focus on the promises and the truths of God's Word and cancel the negative from our thought life. Are you used to having things turn out badly? Do you live in the expectation that the storm cloud over your head will never leave? Cancel this thought process!

The Word of God is filled with H.O.P.E. = Happiness Overtakes with Positive Expectation.

Faith, as I am presenting it here, is positive expectation. This faith is not to be confused with positive thinking. Positive thinking is a work of your soul; positive expectation (Faith) is a work of the Spirit; a Spirit-to-spirit work.

This expectation is spiritual energy, which draws to us that which we are expecting. What I am attempting to say here is what Paul said 2,000 years ago:

> *Now Faith is the substance* (title deed) *of things hoped for, the evidence of things not* (yet) *seen.* Hebrews 11:1 - parentheses mine

Ella Fitzgerald wrote and recorded a song on this subject. The words are straight to the point and good to put before us DAILY until they become habit:

"You got to accentuate the positive,
Eliminate the negative and latch on to the affirmative
Don't mess with mister in-between.
You got to spread joy up to the maximum,
Bring gloom down to the minimum,

Have faith, or pandemonium liable to walk upon the scene."

"To illustrate my last remark
Jonah in the whale, Noah in the ark,
What did they do, just when everything looked so dark?
Man, they said, we better
Accentuate the positive, eliminate the negative,
Latch on to the affirmative don't mess with mister in-between."

Let's look at the story in Numbers (Chapters 12-14) where Moses sent out twelve men to look at the land that had been promised to Israel, The Promised Land. When these men returned to Moses they gave their report. Ten of the twelve thought it was impossible – that the people were too many and too strong. Hear what Caleb and Joshua had to say:

> *And Caleb stilled the people before Moses, and said, "Let us go up at once, and possess it; for we are well able to overcome it."* Numbers 13:30 (KJV)

> *And Joshua the son of Nun, and Caleb the son of Jephunneh, which were of them that searched the land, rent their clothes: And they spake unto all the company of the children of Israel, saying, "The land, which we passed through to search it, is an exceeding good land. If the LORD delight in us, then he will bring us into this land, and give it us; a land which floweth with milk and honey."* Numbers 14:6-8 (KJV)

Caleb and Joshua saw exactly what the other men saw, but they saw with eyes that expected to receive what God had promised them. Yes, eventually they DID receive their promise – no other adult in the assembly that day received the PROMISE. The promise was held for the next generation; the promise was not canceled only postponed.

My Father, used to say (in jest), *"Don't confuse me with the facts, I've got my mind made up."* And *"Some minds are like concrete, all mixed up and thoroughly set."*

Think of your mind as an enhanced video player, with memory and imagination. As we remember events and imagine outcomes, we become emotionally involved. This union causes us to see a thing as accomplished. Our brain doesn't know the difference in our imagination, what we see with our natural eyes, or what we see with our FAITH eyes. If our brain sees it, our body reacts to it and our belief/expectation is kindled.

Don't believe me? Next time you go to a movie, tell me your body and emotions don't react to what you see on screen, even though you know it is not reality. Yes, movies and books move us to laughter, tears, anger, fear and more. I remember watching my father get fully involved in a fistfight while watching the TV western *Gun Smoke*. My son and my husband jump, scream and run around when watching a football game on television.

Mental agreement (a renewed mind in unity to the Word of God) to the promises of God is a vital ingredient in receiving. You don't have to understand it to mentally agree with the Word of God. He will bring the understanding.

WE DRAW TO US WHAT WE BELIEVE (EXPECT)

I am fully persuaded that if I focus on THE PROBLEM (where I am, what I don't have, how I have failed) that is all I will have. However, if I focus on what God has promised me, really focus; purpose to believe, deliberately and unconditionally, that is what I will have. Deliberate, FOCUSED HOPE – we must focus [a center of interest or activity; closed or narrow attention; concentration] our expectation (hope) **on the One who promised**, NOT just the promise. Real HOPE is a focus on the goodness, faithfulness and dependability of God, the One who made the promise.

"A believer's number one job is to BELIEVE."
Joyce Meyer

Waiting on God is an active state of patient expectation, not a passive state of doing nothing; it is an active attitude of expecting something good:

- Full of expectation
- Full of hope
- In a state of grateful thanksgiving

In God's economy, we have to get it in our heart (our spirit, mind and soul) before we get it in our hand. I know in my heart, not just my head. I know my Redeemer lives. I know my God is good; I know His Word is true – I don't care how I feel or how it looks. Stay positive, expect, be full of hope and happy anticipation. Declare: "I refuse to live in the pit of despair, God is for me, I am His beloved!"

We know the now of my circumstances; God wants to show us the end of the circumstances. Faith eyes and faith heart are not just needed to help us get to that end circumstance; they hold us and keep us focused on Jesus in the in-between time.

"Faith is comprised of 3 things:

1) *Facts to be believed,*
2) *Commands to be obeyed*
3) *Promises to be enjoyed"*

--A. E. Mellors

More Scriptures to memorize

These build your faith in a faithful God when your circumstances say otherwise:

I would have despaired unless I had believed that I would see the goodness of the LORD in the land of the living. (Psalm 27:13)

Behold, the eye of the LORD is on those who fear Him, on those who hope for His lovingkindness. (Psalm 33:18)

And now, Lord, for what do I wait? My hope is in You. (Psalm 39:7)

Why are you in despair, O my soul? And why are you disturbed within me? Hope in God, for I shall again praise Him, The help of my countenance and my God. (Psalm 43:5)

The steadfast of mind You will keep in perfect peace, Because he trusts in You. (Isaiah 26:3)

For Sheol cannot thank You, Death cannot praise You; those who go down to the pit cannot hope for Your faithfulness. (Isaiah 38:18)

Yet those who wait for the LORD will gain new strength; They will mount up with wings like eagles, They will run and not get tired, They will walk and not become weary. (Isaiah 40:31)

If a man dies, will he live again? All the days of my struggle I will wait until my change comes. (Job 14:14, NAS)

WHICH IS BIGGER?

All fear, all threats, and all intimidation say, "Bow your knee to me, for I am greater than God." You have to decide which is bigger and more powerful: the problem or GOD. I am certainly not saying that EVERYTHING we fear will be drawn to us, but what we concentrate on, we believe. What we believe, we become emotionally involved in, and that involvement pulls into our life that thing. Worse yet, fear is torment, and that is not healthy energy in which to live.

"For the thing which I fear cometh upon me, and that which I am afraid of cometh unto me." Job 3:25 (NAS)

Since what we see around us originally came from the realm we cannot see, as children of the Most High God, what we say, what we think, and how we live affects our life in super-powerful ways (good and bad) and pulls from that unseen realm.

There is no fear in love; but perfect love casteth out fear: because fear hath torment. He that feareth is not made perfect in love. I John 4:18 (KJV)

Receiving and giving out the Love of God leaves no room in our finite minds for destructive, negative expectations. The operational Love of God falls under the categories of forgiveness, unity, generosity and humility.

A TRUE STORY OF EXPECTANT FAITH

I know a young woman who had been in a multi-year legal battle with her ex-husband over custody of their children. He seemed to have unlimited funds to take her before the judge for one trumped-up reason after another. She finally got to a place where she had exhausted her and her family's financial reserve to pay attorney fees to represent her each time.

Last year he filed a petition for full custody (again). She called her family and called on God. She and her mother decided that they would appear at court, as summoned, without representation and expect God to take care of the situation however He chose. They prayed together and had trusted friends praying.

When they showed up for court, as they walked into the courthouse, they ran into an attorney friend who had just moved back to town and was there to represent someone in a different case. After hugs and small talk, he asked what they were doing there. He then asked who was representing them. When they told him no one, he was shocked, and said, "You can't go before a judge unrepresented! Tell me when and where and I will finish what I am doing and I will come represent you for FREE." They expected, God supplied, AND they prevailed. Case Closed! (excuse the pun). Plus, when the ex-husband's attorney saw that his client had been lying, he resigned and refused to ever represent him again.

God has infinite ways of meeting our needs. He has vast resources. More importantly – He wants to! Most of the time we don't ask; if we ask we don't expect. Beloved, it is faith that moves what you need and what you have been promised from God (the Spirit realm) to you (the natural realm). Begging, crying, reasoning and bargaining do not work.

> *Let those who favor my righteous cause and have pleasure in my uprightness shout for joy and be glad and say continually, Let the Lord be magnified, Who takes pleasure in the prosperity of His servant.* Psalm 35:27 (Amplified)

The word prosperity in this scripture is translated from the Old Testament Hebrew word *Shalom* meaning: Completeness, soundness, well-being. It is used when one asks or prays for the welfare of another. It can mean material prosperity or physical safety or spiritual well-being. God takes pleasure in our completeness, soundness, well being (physical and spiritual), our material prosperity and our physical safety. That is what this scripture says. The Word of God is the TRUTH; believe it and expect it to produce. God actually wants us to PROSPER.

Several years ago my husband changed jobs and we needed to sell our house to move from Alabama to Louisiana. Houses in our town were selling well, yet ours was NOT; it wasn't even showing. It had been on the market six months! Plus, when we put the house on the market, I gave my 60-day notice, knowing that by the time the school year was finished, our house would be sold, and I would only be unemployed for 30 days at most.

One afternoon I went up to the church to pray (as if location made a difference), and instead of prayer, I began to reason with God and beg Him. He spoke clearly to my spirit and said, "Linda, you don't have to beg." I can tell you that when God speaks that clearly and directly to you, it will make you sit up straight and pay attention. He is so very gentle and good – He understands our frailties and our misconceptions. Our house sold about three months later, and in retrospect, His timing was perfect.

~ ~ ~ ~ ~ ~ ~

Turn that stinkin' thinkin' around! God responds to faith, not begging, not bargaining, not even tears. God will not move faster because we are miserable, pitiful, crying, or depressed. Only faith (positive expectation – focused hope) pleases and motivates God. Our faith pleases him.

Another benefit of faith is REST. When you are in faith, you aren't ringing your hands and in a state of anxious worry. You can speak to your fearful mind and say, "God has this situation well in hand, and I will stay busy doing those things for which I am responsible – instead of being disabled by despair."

> *"Are you tired? Worn out? Burned out on religion? Come to me. Get away with me and you'll recover your life. I'll show you how to take a real rest. Walk with me and work with me—watch how I do it. Learn the unforced rhythms of grace. I won't lay anything heavy or ill-fitting on you. Keep company with me and you'll learn to live freely and lightly."* Matt. 11:28-30 (The Message)

Again, I ask which is bigger, beloved, God or the problem? You can stay busy looking at the problem, talking about the problem, and wringing your hands over the problem. These are all passive activities that get you more of the same. OR, you can determine to let God teach you to trust Him.

RESTORE SCRIPTURES TO MEMORIZE

He makes me lie down in green pastures, he leads me beside quiet waters. (Psalm 23:2)

Be still before the LORD and wait patiently for him; do not fret when men succeed in their ways, when *they carry out their wicked schemes.* (Psalm 37:7)

Be at rest once more, O my soul, for the LORD has been good to you. (Psalm 116:7)

In vain you rise early and stay up late, toiling for food to eat—for He grants sleep to those He loves. (Psalm 127:2)

I know that the LORD secures justice for the poor and upholds the cause of the needy. (Psalm 140:12)

The fear of the LORD leads to life: Then one rests content, untouched by trouble. (Proverbs 19:23)

FLESH OR SPIRIT?

The Secret of Humility

> *Abraham, remember, had two sons: one by the slave woman and one by the free woman. The son of the slave woman was born by human connivance; the son of the free woman was born by God's promise. This illustrates the very thing we are dealing with now. The two births represent two ways of being in relationship with God.* Galatians 4:22-23 (The Message)

The opposite of humility is pride. Not the kind of pride that says, "I am wonderful." Instead, it is the kind that says, "I am not going to bother God with _______ (fill in the blank), I can do it myself." Beloved, we must lay aside this kind of thinking. It is His desire to transfer to us His abilities.

> *From the Catholic Encyclopedia (1913), Humility is defined as, "A quality by which a person considering his own defects has a humble opinion of himself and* ***willingly submits himself to God****. . .Jesus Christ is the ultimate definition of Humility."*

Humility is the foundation of the Spirit-to-spirit structure and inferior only to faith because humility removes the obstacles to faith. It removes pride and makes a man subject to and a fit recipient of grace; and grace is God's power through His Spirit.

"But He gives a greater grace Therefore it says, "GOD IS OPPOSED To THE PROUD, BUT GIVES GRACE TO THE HUMBLE." James 4:6 (NAS)

But know this, we do not labor or put ourselves under some self-imposed discipline or legalistic strategy. No, we yield to a loving Lord each step of the way and we wake up one day to find another facet of His character cut into our Spirit. It is only the power of His grace that removes pride, replacing it with humility.

But the fruit of the Spirit is love, joy, peace, patience, kindness, goodness, faithfulness gentleness, self-control; against such things there is no law.
Galatians 5:22-23 (NAS)

But what happens when we live God's way? He brings gifts into our lives, much the same way that fruit appears in an orchard—things like affection for others, exuberance about life, serenity. We develop a willingness to stick with things, a sense of compassion in the heart, and a conviction that a basic holiness permeates things and people. We find ourselves involved in loyal commitments, not needing to force our way in life, able to marshal and direct our energies wisely.

Legalism is helpless in bringing this about; it only gets in the way. Among those who belong to Christ, everything connected with getting our own way and mindlessly responding to what everyone else calls necessities is killed off for good—crucified.

Since this is the kind of life we have chosen, the life of the Spirit, let us make sure that we do not just hold it as an idea in our heads or a sentiment in our hearts, but work out its implications in every detail of

> *our lives. That means we will not compare ourselves with each other as if one of us were better and another worse. We have far more interesting things to do with our lives. Each of us is an original.* Galatians 5:22-26 (The Message)

These traits cannot become part of the composition of my character solely by an act of my will. Certainly many well-disciplined, strong-willed people can accomplish some of these, but if it is a work of the soul, it is a work of pride. Real, permanent, change (life transformation) comes from the Spirit of God, coupled with my willingness – only. We are not called human doings, we *are* human beings. Religion is a work of the soul. Religion says, "You must do something to become _______." (Fill in the blank with whatever you think God requires of you.) Relationship with your creator says, "I made you, so let me help you BE that which I made."

Orange trees do not labor to produce oranges; it is a genetic factor which flows from the essence of the tree. We Christians have a new genetic chain in the Spirit that is now connected to the mighty Holy Spirit. It is from that genetic material all this and more will be accomplished. We must train our minds to believe (see what is in) our Spirit. Our Spirit is now connected to God (a high speed, wireless connection). He is the truth; He is in charge, NOT our mind. Choose to actively change your conscious mind, and the subconscious will follow. Not only that, you will be pulling the PROMISE from the unseen realm into the seen realm. I can offer you a bonus to this: believing God gives you favor. "Faith pleases God" (Hebrews 11:6).

ILLUSTRATION: FLESH OR SPIRIT

An aging Indian Chief decided to take his only grandson on a walking hunting trip with the purpose of sharing wisdom and beginning to train him in the care of the tribe. For several days they walked, fished, hunted, made tools, and talked about God's great plan for his life, the tribe, and the lands. The boy listened, asked many good questions, and learned much from his beloved grandfather.

On the last night together before returning to the tribe, the grandfather said, "I have one more important thing you must know in order to lead and accomplish God's plan for you and this people. My son, there are two great wolves inside you, and they are at war. They are fighting for the right to rule you. One is wise and good; the other is evil and manipulative." Then the chief sat silently.

The grandson thought about this for a while and then asked, "Grandfather, which one wins?"

"The one you feed, my son," the grandfather replied. "The one you feed."

No place for flesh – all Spirit. Our humble position says, "I need God to accomplish <u>(fill in the blank).</u> What it DOES NOT say is, "I am lowly; I am no better than a worm; I am not worthy." We have already covered the part where God has made us His child, and our faith gives us favor with Him. Let me add to this by saying, we are accepted among the Beloved (Ephesians 1:6); God has poured out His love in our hearts (Romans 5:5); NOTHING can separate us from the Love of God (Romans 8:39). This is nothing to be proud of or boast about because it is not something we have done; it is something God has made us to be.

> *He chose the lowly things of this world and the despised things—and the things that are not—to nullify the things that are, so that no one may boast before him. It is because of him that you are in Christ Jesus, who has become for us wisdom from God—that is, our righteousness, holiness and redemption. Therefore, as it is written: "Let him who boasts boast in the Lord.*
> 1 Corinthians 1:28-31 (NIV)

Humility ALSO means to prefer others, to be gracious and cooperative, to be thick skinned (not easily offended), and to cut out the selfish ambitions and vain imaginations. In short, ditch the pride. What exactly do we have to be proud about? He has done and is doing this great work in us; all we have done is submit to the process. I do not see any room for big talk or swagger.

Jesus is our example in that He NEVER demanded His own way, but was "in charge" when necessary. He NEVER defended Himself, but He defended the sacred things of God at the Temple. His daily life was NEVER about Him; it was about establishing the Kingdom of God by submitting to His Father's directions.

Humility cannot be fabricated or taught. It is part of a genetic change accomplished in our soul by The Holy Spirit. You can receive this change of character through the grace flow of His Holy Spirit. It begins with a willing heart and eventually becomes natural, from the Spirit realm to the physical realm – Spirit to spirit.

> *. . .Agree with each other, love each other, be deep-spirited friends. Don't push your way to the front; don't sweet-talk your way to the top. Put yourself aside, and help others get ahead. Don't be obsessed with getting your own advantage. Forget yourselves long enough to lend a helping hand.* Philippians 2:1-4 (The Message)

Our Fuel

The Living Word

> *For the word of God is living and active. Sharper than any double-edged sword, it penetrates even to dividing soul and Spirit, joints and marrow; it judges the thoughts and attitudes of the heart.* Hebrews 4:12 (NIV)

We choose to allow the Word of God to divide soul and Spirit. It is a process and it is a choice, beloved. The soul believes what has been, what it knows from what it sees. We must train it to receive new, positive information. EXPECT THE PROMISE, not the dreaded *it never, I always, I can't, but how?!*

The battle between soul and Spirit is a form of spiritual warfare. We can win these battles by just recognizing that the struggle exists. Our sins and addictions are still a powerful force, but they can no longer control us unless we allow it. The first step to overcoming is realizing that we are powerless over them; by accepting Jesus Christ as our Lord and Savior we are more than conquerors. Only God can heal us and restore our focus. There is no injury so great, no addiction so absolute that the grace of God cannot overcome.

I wrote earlier that prior to becoming a Christian, our soul ruled our life. When our spirit is in charge, our mind, our will, and our emotions (our soul) becomes faith-focused.

> *Now faith is the (substance) assurance (the confirmation, the title deed) of the things [we] hope for, being the proof of things [we] do not see and the*

conviction of their reality [faith perceiving as real fact what is not revealed to the senses]. For by faith, [trust and holy fervor born of faith] the men of old had divine testimony borne to them and obtained a good report.

By faith we understand that the worlds [during the successive ages] were framed [fashioned, put in order, and equipped for their intended purpose] by the word of God, so that what we see was not made out of things which are visible.

But without faith it is impossible to please and be satisfactory to Him. For whoever would come near to God must [necessarily] believe that God exists and that He is the rewarder of those who earnestly and diligently seek Him [out].

Because of faith also Sarah herself received physical power to conceive a child, even when she was long past the age for it, because she considered [God] Who had given her the promise to be reliable and trustworthy and true to His word. So from one man, though he was physically as good as dead, there have sprung descendants whose number is as the stars of heaven and as countless as the innumerable sands on the seashore. Hebrews 11:1-12 (excerpts from the Amplified Bible, emphasis mine)

Yes, we must make deliberate, conscious choices. When these new conscious principles become natural choices, then the subconscious follows suit. Circumstances can result from choices; choices are a result of thoughts. Your thought life is a powerful instrument in your living environment. Fear (worry), for example, can be so hidden in your thought life that, as a result, your body lives in a constant state of stress. Studies have shown that the "Fight or Flight Response" is slowly, physically killing our bodies.

WHAT IS THE "FIGHT OR FLIGHT RESPONSE?

This fundamental physiologic response forms the foundation of modern day stress medicine. The fight or flight response is our body's primitive, automatic, inborn response that prepares the body to "fight" or "flee" from perceived attack, harm or threat to our survival. What happens to us when we are under excessive stress?

> *When we experience excessive stress—whether from internal worry or external circumstance—a bodily reaction is triggered, called the "fight or flight" response. Originally discovered by the great Harvard physiologist Walter Cannon, this response is hard-wired into our brains and represents a genetic wisdom designed to protect us from bodily harm. This response actually corresponds to an area of our brain called the hypothalamus, which—when stimulated—initiates a sequence of nerve cell firing and chemical release that prepares our body for running or fighting.* (Neil F. Neimark, M.D)

Every time your body triggers this fight or flight response for situations that are not truly life-threatening, you are experiencing, in effect, a false alarm. Too many false alarms can lead to stress-related disorders like heart disease, high blood pressure, immune system disorders, migraine headaches, insomnia, and sexual dysfunction.

Fear is the root of this response. As you seek to uncover the root fear, ask God to reveal it to you. Then repent, release and rest in God's hope and provision for the circumstances. Like all new habits, you will have to repeat this process over and over. It also requires you allowing Him, by the power of His grace, to do the necessary healing to that root area of your past.

Often our body is under attack because we have chosen to hear the reports of doom and gloom and give them more validity than the Word of God. Remember, previously we talked about agreement? Are we in agreement with the reports? Yes, there is reality – bad things really do happen. Our trust in Him, however, can often make substantial changes to the real world in which we live. Where do these reports come from?

- Daily news
- Doctors
- Teachers
- Pastors
- Co-workers
- Family
- Books
- Television
- Movies
- Friends

I believe it is important to know what is going on in the world around us personally, locally, nationally, and internationally. I have a friend who reads the paper and watches the news so he can gain direction for daily prayer. News stories are reported from the perspective of the person reporting it or the dictates of their superiors. All news is slanted, but the truth and/or the agenda can be gleaned from it if you view it through the eyes of the Spirit.

Many journalist and editors think of themselves as prophets and preachers. They promote their own agenda and pronounce their own predictions based on their life beliefs and views. I know that I sound cynical, but I assure you I am not – I am one who listens to what is said and then takes it to God in prayer, especially if I hear or see anything that brings fear. God's agenda and plan hold my utmost interest.

For God hath not given us a spirit of fear; but of power and of love and of a sound mind. I Timothy 1:7 (KJV)

I am not suggesting we should toss out all common sense. Common sense to a spirit ruled person is above and beyond regular, mental common sense. That is how we should function as Spirit influenced people. What I am suggesting is that we turn fear into our tool, and not our enemy. Certainly we should go to the doctor for our annual physical and when we aren't feeling well. I know people that stay in a state of obsession over their health and run after every new miracle trend in the market. Where is the peace in that? Where is the faith in that? And when we get an unfavorable diagnosis, we need to take that to Jesus, too. Everything is subject to change, and change is subject to Jesus.

I read books, watch television and movies, and socialize with a diverse group of people. I am careful what I watch and read. The Word of God says to

Let your speech be always with grace, seasoned with salt, that ye may know how ye ought to answer every man. Colossians 4:6 (KJV, emphasis mine)

Therefore, I should flavor all social gatherings with the presence of a loving Savior and not the other way around. I am not talking about being this hyper-religious, scripture-quoting, self-righteous person – be humble and normal. At the same time, do not allow the negative and selfish attitudes of the people around to influence you. God did not call us to be locked up in a remote monastery away from the world. He has asked us to live in such a way that His Spirit is predominant in all our dealings. His Spirit is not namby-pamby; His Spirit in us is in peaceful dominion everywhere we go. His Spirit in us = DOMINION! That means the Lord God is in charge, so everywhere we take Him, we take His dominion.

At a conference held in January 2008 called "Starting The Year Off Right," Dutch Sheets said,

> *When we expand our thinking to a Kingdom world view everything is going to change because every situation we step into we are going to realize that we are there to extend the dominion of God in that place. We are going to begin to live in the Lord's prayer, '"Thy Kingdom come, Thy will be done on earth as it is in heaven..."' we aren't going to be earthbound any longer in our thinking – we are going to move into a realm of revelation that moves us far above anything we have known before. We are going to be dangerous Kingdom people wherever we go.*

Beloved, since we are connected Spirit-to-spirit with our creator God, we are literally carriers of the presence and glory of God. We have within us the atmosphere of faith, the realm where the impossible is made possible. We have within us the sweet love of God to heal, save and set free. We were pre-wired for power before we were born (The Deposit). However, that power grid was not connected to the power source, because we were born in sin. When we became His and gave our lives to Him, His Spirit connected to our spirit, and the power (everything we need) began to flow.

Visualize our faith as this: Jesus is the power-generating unit but we are the wires transmitting the power to where it is needed. We don't have the power, Jesus does. But, He depends on us to deliver it. When we are born again, we all have a measure of faith which is the same measure as Jesus. But we have to start believing in the ability of Jesus to answer our prayers and exercising our faith. In our example, consider us as starting out with (and having the wisdom to handle) 120 volt faith, which is the same as having the ability to power a light bulb or small appliance. By exercising our faith, we can graduate to the 240 volt faith which can then power the air conditioning system. Then we can move up the ladder to industrial strength faith to power large industrial motors of 4160 volts or 6900 volts. Or, we can kick it up a notch and graduate to the 500,000 volt high tension wires coming off a nuclear power plant. When you pass these high tension wires on the road, say to yourself, "That's me." That's when you know you can heal the sick, raise the dead, change the weather, and change the course of history. When we hear or read about these great people of faith that do these things, think to yourself, "Why not me?" And then Jesus will respond, "I can use all the recruits I can get. Go for it!"

His Word is the fuel that transforms my soul into a container of His Faith. Faith has substance; it is energy that translates God's provision and promises from the Spirit Realm into the physical realm. Isaac actually existed before he was born to Abraham and Sarah. Abraham's unfailing faith in the integrity of God and His promise did not create Isaac, but brought him to this life.

In October 1980 when I became a Christian, a teacher in my church counseled me to read the Bible daily. Not out of obligation or need for intellectual growth, but because, he said, "You have a newborn Spirit in you which must be fed Spiritual food. Just as a newborn baby needs physical nutrition to grow strong, without proper nutrition, you will be weak and vulnerable."

Beloved, the Word of God is living, spiritual fuel for growth and vitality (mental, emotional, physical, financial and spiritual). His Word is alive and working in you!

> *In the beginning was the Word, and the Word was with God, and the Word was God. The same was in the beginning with God. All things were made by him; and without him was not any thing made that was made. In him was life; and the life was the light of men.* John 1:1-4 (KJV)

Never forget His Word is alive. Allow it to feed your spirit. Ask the Spirit of God to help you understand it – He will.

Our View

The Secret of Perspective

So we fix our eyes not on what is seen, but on what is unseen. For what is seen is temporary but what is unseen is eternal. II Corinthians 4:18

What then is our perspective to be?

We can look at our flaws, our limitations, and circumstances, or we can look at the goodness and vast resources of God.

Both are real both produce.

In 2006 my husband and I took a trip to Costa Rica. As you know, it is a small Central American country about the size of Mississippi. When you are in the central mountains on a clear day looking west, you can see the Pacific Ocean; then looking east, you see mountains, valleys, and beautiful vegetation. They are both real views from the very same location. If you only look east, however, you would not know the ocean was behind you.

I believe that because we live in this natural world and our five senses confirm to our mind that only what we see around us is real, we begin to dismiss any notion that there is anything else.

Our perspective influences our EXPECTATIONS (our faith). We WILL choose to believe either what we see with our natural eyes or what we see with our spirit eyes. If we have come to believe what we see with our natural eyes is the only reality, we must determine to see with new eyes (spirit eyes). Jesus was asked by his disciples, in Matthew 13:11, 13-16, why He taught in parables.

> *And he answered and said unto them, "Unto you it is given to know the mysteries of the kingdom of heaven, but to them it is not given . . . And unto them is fulfilled the prophecy of Isaiah, which saith, '"By hearing ye shall hear, and shall in no wise understand; And seeing ye shall see, and shall in no wise perceive: For this people's heart is waxed gross, And their ears are dull of hearing, And their eyes they have closed; Lest haply they should perceive with their eyes, And hear with their ears, And understand with their heart, And should turn again, And I should heal them."' But blessed are your eyes, for they see; and your ears, for they hear."* (KJV)

This must be intentional at first. This is another one of those wonderful opportunities where we get to partner with God to change within. Instead of saying, "I can't!" say, "How can I?" Ask Him to give your spirit sight – revelation of His plan on any circumstance.

I know a woman whose son and daughter-in-law divorced. She had a promise from God that the curse of divorce had been removed from her family. She stands firm on His promise. She recognizes that the divorce has taken place, but knows God will restore. There is nothing she can do; restoration is His plan and His responsibility. Her focus is on praise and worship to Him and refusing to look on the ongoing circumstances with her natural eyes. She changed her perspective.

I suppose one could do it by an act of self-will, positive thinking, or whatever the going phrase is now, and to be sure, many have. However, I don't believe there is any peace in that or any lasting fruit. Further, and most importantly, if we can do it, why do we need Him – pride is the product of this kind of act. Pride separates me from my loving Lord and His power.

Here is one of the ways I pray: "Lord, you know what I see, and you know what I hear, and you know what is going on. I come to you in need of a new perspective. I need your view on the circumstances, your wisdom, and your direction." I also go to His Word on the matter. How He directs me is how I pray and stand. Each and every time my mind looks at the situation, I make an intentional mental shift – like changing the channel on the radio. If I don't have a specific word on the matter, I thank Him for His faithfulness and His goodness.

> *Set your minds on things above, not on earthly things.*
> Colossians 3:2 (NIV)

> *Do not let this Book of the Law depart from your mouth; meditate on it day and night, so that you may be careful to do everything written in it. Then you will be prosperous and successful.* Joshua 1:8 (NIV)

Beloved, living a life of dread is no way to live. Living a life believing and having faith in the goodness and faithfulness of our Lord is a life of rest, liberty and abundance. It's not magic; it's authenticity.

"O soul, are you weary and troubled?
No light in the darkness you see?
There's light for a look at the Savior,
and life more abundant and free!
Turn your eyes upon Jesus,
look full in His wonderful face,
and the things of earth will grow strangely dim
in the light of His Glory and Grace."

Helen H. Lemmel (1863-1961) "Turn Your Eyes Upon Jesus" (1922)

This beautiful hymn, "Turn Your Eyes Upon Jesus," was written by a blind woman, Helen Lemmel. The heart of worship doesn't just come out of good circumstances; it also comes from a heart that knows the love and faithfulness of the Lord God. Being blind is a circumstance, not an identity. Sight and hearing do not guarantee proper perspective.

However, most often we view who we are by our circumstances and life experiences. Since we have been moved from the kingdom of this world into The Kingdom of God, we are a NEW creation, with new Divine Spirit DNA. Who we are is now determined by God and what His word says about us.

"We cannot pray with power, confidence and authority if our line-of-sight is only what we see taking place around us."

Garris Elkins

WORTHY?

Do you find yourself asking, "Am I really worthy?" This is a shame issue. Let us look at this briefly. We have all been introduced to shame in our lives. What I call normal shame comes when I have done something wrong or something poorly. Abnormal shame, however, comes and says, "You are wrong and you are bad." When I do something wrong, I go to God and ask for His forgiveness – and I RECEIVE forgiveness (I John 1:9). He calls me valuable.

If I were asked to catch a football and run for a touchdown ahead of the rest of the team, I would fail miserably. That failure wouldn't diminish my value or my worth as a person; it would simply prove I am not a football player. You are who God says you are, NOT your circumstances, NOT your past, NOT your abilities or disabilities. Beloved, do not put the condition of worthiness on your capacity to receive from God or your ability to move in His behalf. The root is false humility, which is pride (again).

. . .giving thanks to the Father, who has qualified us to share in the inheritance of the saints in light.
Colossians 1:2 (NAS)

He made us worthy. He qualified us to share in the inheritance! Simply put, the Secret of God is a spirit work in us, a gift of God, established in us, purchased for us by the work done, price paid by Jesus 2,000 years ago on Calvary. This is a FINISHED fact, accomplished the day we were born again regardless of how we feel from day to day.

"Dare to stand in the presence of sense-knowledge-facts, and declare that you are what God says you are."

E. W. Kenyon

Set some time aside, just you and your Lord. Get a tablet and a pen. Ask God to show you what He thinks about you. He will show you in His Word. Buy a concordance and start looking up words and the corresponding scriptures. List them, confess them! Ask God to pull up your antenna so you can hear the good others see in you – write it down. Focus on your accomplishments, sharpen areas that are weak, as He directs and enables.

Replace the established facts with the TRUTH. For example: If people have rejected you, God's Word says that you are *"ACCEPTED among the beloved"* Ephesians 1:6 (KJV, emphasis mine); if you live in fear or confusion, God's Word says, *"For God hath not given us the spirit of fear; but of power, and of love, and of a sound mind"* II Timothy 1:7 (KJV). The truth of God is greater than the facts of any situation.

God has a plan for your life (Jeremiah 29:11), a good plan (many plans). This is not Plan B. It is not something He came up with now that you have been moved into His Kingdom. **This plan was made a part of you when you were made.** He has provided all the tools for you to accomplish this plan and does the work in you to make those tools fully operational, if you are willing.

I don't believe Abraham ever doubted God. I think he tried to help Him once or twice, but he never doubted. I believe Abraham saw Isaac every time he looked up into the night sky, filled with stars. Plus, in the process of waiting on the promise, God blessed Abraham in many ways. Abraham was not a poor man and not ashamed to receive from God.

Sit down with a notebook and ask yourself these questions:

1) Does Jesus have limitations? Yes or No. If so, what are they?
2) Was the price paid by Jesus Christ at Calvary enough (for me)?
3) Is it selfish to ask for God's promises, provision and blessings and then receive what God has promised? King David did not think it selfish: *"And now it has pleased You to bless the house of Your servant, that it may continue forever before You; for You, O LORD, have blessed, and it is blessed forever."* I Chronicles 17:27 (NAS)
4) Ask God to show you His perspective on your life and your prayer list.
5) Is the grace of God *really* powerful enough to heal and deliver me?

Again, I want to encourage you to find a Bible with a concordance, find out how God feels about you and how much He loves you, then write them down, say them out loud every day until you accept the truth of them in your heart. I will get you started with Ephesians 1:3-6 (The Message):

How blessed is God! And what a blessing he is! He's the Father of our Master, Jesus Christ, and takes us to the high places of blessing in him. Long before he laid down earth's foundations, he had us in mind, had settled on us as the focus of his love, to be made whole and holy by his love. Long, long ago he decided to adopt us into his family through Jesus Christ. (What pleasure he took in planning this!) He wanted us to enter into the celebration of his lavish gift-giving by the hand of his beloved Son.

Not long ago, I was watching an interview of Oprah Winfrey where she was talking about meeting with the first girls chosen to start the school she had built in Africa. She said she sat down with them and allowed them to ask questions about her, why she did this or just anything they wanted to know. Then, when finished, she began to ask them questions. Picking a girl who had asked her many questions, she said, "Tell me about you, who are you?" Oprah said the young girl bowed her head and said, "Oh, I am just a poor girl." Oprah, gently lifted her chin, looked into her eyes, and said, "Poverty is a circumstance, not an identity!"

But thou, O LORD, art a shield for me; my glory, and the lifter up of mine head. Psalm 3:3 (KJV)

The secret of perspective is to change our view from the problem to the only solution, the only answer, Jesus. We must also turn our eyes from what we think about ourselves to what He says we are and the work accomplished by Him to qualify us to walk in what He says we are. We tolerate poor perspective on life and on ourselves; more importantly we tolerate unbelief. Let us make a conscious decision to seek Him for a new perspective and believe Him until it is visible.

As for me I say, "God is who He says He is,
God can do what He says He can do,
I am who God says I am,
I can do all things through Christ,
who strengthens me,
The Word of God is alive and working in me."

Beth Moore
Believing God

Turn Your Worry Into Worship, Your Gripes Into Gratitude

The Secret of Gratitude and Generosity

Be anxious for nothing, but in everything by prayer and supplication with thanksgiving let your requests be made known to God. Philippians 4:6

The secret of Gratitude and Generosity are separate, but function as one. They are not like two sides of the same coin, but they are individuals that are connected and cannot be separated – like conjoined twins. You cannot be grateful without being generous or be generous without gratitude. Even though they are different, they operate in unity.

"Worry can be compared to a rocking chair; it will keep you busy, but it won't get you anywhere."

M. Lee McClary

Worry, I believe, is worse, so much worse. I believe that we pull negative things into our life by BELIEVING and EXPECTING bad things – *negative faith.* Worry ruins the present, affects our attitudes, our digestion, and our sleep. It is noise pollution in your head. Worry never changes the circumstances, and most of the time what we worry about (fear) never happens unless we begin to believe it – *negative faith*. We start picturing what is coming, our mind sees it as reality, connects it to our emotions, and our emotions create our belief; our expectation, our faith.

Worship, on the other hand, is positive for our mind, our emotions, our body, and our spirit. Worship cleans the poisons from our soul. Worship also brings God into the circumstances, which is where you will find the solution to any problem. Second Chronicles chapter 20 tells the story of when the Moabites and Ammonites (and) some of the Meunites came to make war on Jehoshaphat; "a vast army." Jehoshaphat did not run around hysterically, wringing his hands and crying to everyone that came to his house. He just *"resolved to inquire of the LORD, and he proclaimed a fast for all Judah. The people of Judah came together to seek help from the LORD. . . Then Jehoshaphat stood up in the assembly of Judah and Jerusalem at the temple of the LORD . . .* (and prayed)."

> *Then the Spirit of the LORD came upon Jahaziel. . .* (and he said to the assembly), *"Listen, King Jehoshaphat and all who live in Judah and Jerusalem! This is what the LORD says to you. 'Do not be afraid or discouraged because of this vast army. For the battle is not yours, but God's. . .'"*

Then God told them where to find the enemy and exactly what to do.

> *Go out to face them tomorrow, and the LORD will be with you. . .* (Early the next morning) *Jehoshaphat stood and said, "Listen to me, Judah and people of Jerusalem! Have faith in the LORD your God and you will be upheld. . ."* (Then,) *"Jehoshaphat appointed men to sing to the LORD and to praise him for the splendor of his holiness as they went out at the head of the army, saying: "Give thanks to the LORD, for his love endures forever." As they began to sing and*

> *praise, the LORD set ambushes against the men of Ammon and Moab and Mount Seir. . .* (and defeated them).

Praise and worship, flowing from a grateful heart, is a mighty weapon. What seems like only singing and adoration in the natural realm turns into thermonuclear weapons in the Spirit realm.

> *Though the fig tree does not bud and there are no grapes on the vines, though the olive crop fails and the fields produce no food, though there are no sheep in the pen and no cattle in the stalls, yet I will rejoice in the LORD, I will be joyful in God my Savior.*
> Habakkuk 3:17-18 (NIV)

"The act of praising implies the closest fellowship with the One who is being praised. Therefore, praise not merely expresses but completes the enjoyment; it is its appointed consummation. . . In commanding us to glorify Him, God is inviting us to enjoy Him."

C. S. Lewis, Reflections on the Psalms, 1958, p.95

I have a friend who shared a testimony with me regarding praise. She and her husband are hard-working and giving people. He went for a short period of time unemployed, so during this time, finances were slim. They came home one evening to find that their power had been shut off. At the opening of business the next day, they were able to get it restored, but that evening their house was cold and they had four small children. Without hesitation, she said they began to praise God – not because of the circumstances, but because He is good and faithful. She then said, "Within a very short period of time, our house started to warm up and we were comfortable the rest of the evening."

Do you think the Apostle Paul knew this?

> *Be anxious for nothing, but in everything by prayer and supplication with thanksgiving let your requests be made known to God. And the peace of God, which surpasses all comprehension, will guard your hearts and your minds in Christ Jesus.* Philippians 4: 6-7 (NAS)

I call the letter to the Philippians, Paul's joy letter. Paul wrote this joy-filled letter from prison, a cold, damp, rodent infested, sewage-filled hole of a place. From this alone we can be sure he understood the power of praise (genuine heart gratitude).

I heard a teaching recently by Bishop T. D. Jakes relating to God's act of deliverance for His people. In Exodus 19:3-6 (below) God tells Moses to remind the people of Israel that He did great things for them in delivering them from Egypt because He had a purpose for them *"to be my treasured possession."* and *"you will be for Me a kingdom of priests and a holy nation."*

Bishop Jakes went on to say that the office (or job) of the Priest was (is) to perform acts of worship to Him, our God.

> *Then Moses went up to God, and the LORD called to him from the mountain and said, "This is what you are to say to the house of Jacob and what you are to tell the people of Israel: 'You yourselves have seen what I did to Egypt, and how I carried you on eagles' wings and brought you to myself. Now if you obey me fully and keep my covenant, then out of all nations you will be my treasured possession. Although the whole earth is mine, you will be for me a kingdom of priests and a*

holy nation.' These are the words you are to speak to the Israelites."

That is powerful, but what does that have to do with us, you ask? Everything! In I Peter 2:9 (NAS) the Christian is called: *"But you are A CHOSEN RACE, A royal PRIESTHOOD, A HOLY NATION, A PEOPLE FOR GOD'S OWN POSSESSION, so that you may proclaim the excellencies of Him who has called you out of darkness into His marvelous light"* (emphasis mine).

Here is your scenario: You wake up in the middle of the night and YOUR MIND says, "But what about this?" or "How can God?" or "What am I going to do when. . .?" That's when you STOP your racing mind and say something like this:

I thank you, Lord, that you are Lord. You, oh Lord, are wonderful and perfect; You are precious and good. You are the living Word, You are the TRUTH and everything else is a lie. The enemy has come to steal, kill and destroy, but You, Lord, have come to bring abundant life (John 10:10/paraphrased). I choose to trust You and Your Word. I thank You that I can let my concerns be made know to You and rest.

Tell Him your needs and go back to sleep.

Beloved, The Word works in you to do the work God called you to do. Add to that the power and the authority you have been given to speak to and CHANGE your mind; the power and the authority to speak to and SILENCE your enemy. This makes you dangerous. We must CHOOSE to operate in that authority! In doing so, OPEN your mouth; it must be spoken. It is essential; I cannot stress this point enough. Further, I am not just saying you have authority, I will prove it in the Word, which is the foundation of this and all creation.

1) *In my vision at night I looked, and there before me was one like a son of man, coming with the clouds of heaven. He approached the Ancient of Days and was led into his presence. He (Jesus) was given authority, glory and sovereign power; all peoples, nations and men of every language worshiped him. His dominion is an everlasting dominion that will not pass away, and his kingdom is one that will never be destroyed.* Daniel 7:13-14 (NIV)

2) [Jesus Sends Out the Twelve] *Then Jesus went around teaching from village to village. Calling the Twelve to him, He sent them out two by two and (Jesus) gave them authority over evil* [Greek unclean] *Spirits.* Mark 6:7 (NIV, parentheses mine)

THE SECRET OF GRATITUDE

Here is your new scenario: Get up, every morning, with praise in your heart – proceeding out of your mouth. You woke up, right? Well, thank Him! Did you wake up in your right mind? Thank Him! Thank Him for the bed you slept in. Get a notebook, date a new page every day and write down your gratitude list. Don't copy the day before, make a NEW list every day. CHOOSE to make gratitude a habit. Thank Him daily for the items on this list. Concentrate on what you have and want, NOT what you don't have, NOT on the problem. Looking at the problem will not bring you joy, and it will NOT solve your problem; WORSE, it can bring more of the same to you.

Do you have a relationship problem? Find good things about that person and thank God for them. Write down the things you appreciate about them. Thank them for these things – yes, open your mouth and tell them. If necessary, forgive them and release then in your prayer time. Yes, you can! The grace of God will empower you to do that which you cannot.

The Secret of Gratitude works in that the more grateful you are the more good comes to you. I am not making this up. You tell people how much you appreciate them, and they will always be willing to do more and more for you. People and good things gravitate to an attitude of gratitude not a sour, grumpy person.

Gratitude also is expressed by how you treat the things and people in your life. Are you grateful for your job? Do it well, God will honor you. Do you hate your job? Do it well, God will honor you. Do you need a job? Find volunteer work while looking for that job and do it well, God will honor you. We are strategically placed by God – He orders our steps (Psalm 37:23). Let us be about finding ways to be the hidden treasure were we live and work.

Do you want a better house or better car or better body? Are you taking care of the one you have? Have you asked God for what you want (James 4)? I am fully persuaded that the God of creation has unlimited resources and great plans for us, but we don't expect them; we expect a limited life. We expect to just get by, and that is what we get. Is it false humility that causes us to LIMIT God? Yes, I believe so. Precious one, how are we to do the work of the Kingdom in the world He placed us in without His power and His resources?

Do you work or live with grumpy, mean-spirited people? Do not concentrate on them, or what is distressing about them. Concentrate instead on blessing them in your prayer time. Do you know if you bless them and they are unable to receive it, that blessing will come back on you (Luke 10:5-6)? Please also remember, you have been given the authority to speak to the spirits in and around these grumpy folks to be silent and still in your presence. Do that, too!

> *No weapon that is formed against you will prosper; and every tongue that accuses you in judgment you will condemn. This is the heritage of the servants of the LORD, "And their vindication is from Me," declares the LORD.* Isaiah 54:17 (NIV)

You don't have to wait for perfection to be grateful, either. I know a person who, regardless of what she has, is never fully happy with it because it isn't the best, the most expensive, or made by the right designer. Life is never satisfying as long as you compare what you have to your idea of perfection. Waiting on perfection to be grateful for your lot will be a long and unsatisfying wait.

THE SECRET OF GENEROSITY

Gratitude is also expressed in generosity. Grateful people are giving people. Stingy people are unhappy people and they never have enough, regardless of what they have.

Give, and it will be given to you. They will pour into your lap a good measure--pressed down, shaken together, and running over. For by your standard of measure it will be measured to you in return.
Luke 6:36 (NIV)

"For by your standard of measure it will be measured to you in return." I am not making this stuff up; it is the Word of God. The above scripture is straight out of the heart of our Lord. He is saying in the most simple of terms, what you give out is what you can expect back in abundance, regardless of what it is: mercy, love, forgiveness, physical needs, financial needs, emotional needs. Give out, over and above your legal obligations, with a heart of generosity and gratitude, and you will always live in divine abundance, lacking NOTHING.

I can almost hear you saying, "It doesn't work!" I beg to differ with you; it will still work even if your only motive is to get something back. However, when your heart is right the return is super-multiplied. Additionally, you must persist; a garden doesn't produce fruit the day after it is planted. We live in an instant, microwave world. We expect instant gratification. I remember when I first came to know the Lord and found the scripture in Galatians listing the fruit of the spirit and longing for that to be a part of my life. I thought it would never happen. I now have love, joy, peace, patience, kindness, goodness, faithfulness, gentleness, and self-control, but it wasn't instant. God's Spirit planted the seeds in my spirit. I nurtured the seed (His living word) and the seed produced. God's Spirit broods over us and watches over His word to produce a fruit-filled life (Gen. 1:2; Isa. 55:11).

Instant Fruit?

Several years ago my brother worked for a company that required him to travel much of the state of Mississippi and south Louisiana. He lived in central Mississippi, and our mother lived in New Orleans. On one of the trips to New Orleans, he took his 5-year-old daughter, Ashley, with him at the request of our mother. It was early spring and Mother always had a garden. When my brother and niece arrived, someone had just tilled the garden, and Mother had planned for Ashley to help her plant it. They picked out seeds and worked all afternoon. The next morning as soon as Ashley woke up, she ran outside to see the produce in the garden. "She came back inside very disappointed," Mother said. When asked what was wrong, Ashley replied, "Mama Lee, we worked hard all day long and nothing happened." She expected instant flowers and vegetables. She is not alone; we all want instant fruit and instant results.

Therefore, my friend, YOU MUST learn to CONTEND FOR IT! Depending on the situation, it will require determination and tenacity, but work it will! As a matter of fact, the Secret of generosity works even for non-believers. There are many, many wealthy people who just keep getting richer because they just keep giving it away. These are principals that are universal, like gravity. You jump off the top of a building (regardless of who you are) and you WILL fall to the ground.

> *Give, and it shall be given unto you; good measure,* ***pressed down****, and shaken together, and running over, shall men give into your bosom. For with the same*

> *measure that ye mete withal it shall be measured to you again.* Luke 6:38 (KJV, emphasis mine)

Remember, beloved, we are not giving to get, we are giving out of obedience to gain resources to do the work of the Kingdom. Our intention and our expectation in this principal is what distinguishes us from non-believers. Our intention is to promote the Kingdom; not self-promotion. Our expectation is in the truth of the word of God. He says His word will accomplish that which it is sent to accomplish (Isa. 55:11), and it says He will rebuke the devourer for your sakes (Mal. 3:ll). Intention and expectation are the foundation of this principal.

I believe in giving. I haven't always, and as a result, I have lived a never-quite-enough life. Over the past 20-plus years, I have learned that giving always produces a return that is abundantly more than your gift. Over and above that, when you put God in the equation, your return is far-reaching and exceedingly more abundant – but usually not instant.

> *"Bring the whole tithe into the storehouse, that there may be food in my house. Test me in this," says the LORD Almighty, "and see if I will not throw open the floodgates of heaven and pour out so much blessing that you will not have room enough for it."* Malachi 3:10 (NIV)

A long-time friend had a period in her life where she had more days of the month than funds to cover them. Simply put, she (like me) stayed broke. She shared with me how when she decided to start tithing, at the time it was not a logical choice. She told me that she was in church one Sunday during the early days of tithing, when the check she wrote for her tithe would leave her nothing for groceries. She paid her tithe anyway, knowing God knew her circumstances and believing He would be true to His word. On her way out of church that morning, an acquaintance caught up with her and handed her an envelope saying, "God asked me to give this to you today." It was cash, plenty enough to buy groceries.

This is a powerful secret that many Christians do not understand. This is life-changing stuff, my friend. Many of us spend more time meditating on the problem than on His Word; we fellowship with the circumstances instead of fellowshipping with Him. So, stop your whining! God does not feel sorry for us. He is ONLY moved by faith. This kind of faith is simply the choice to have Him do the Spirit-to-spirit work in us which will allow the necessary faith to grow. Stop comparing what you have to what others have. Let's look for ways to give things away and opportunities to be grateful to God and others, SEVERAL TIMES A DAY. Develop the Secret of Generosity and Gratitude; remember, it is your choice and then He will take over.

Set Apart For Good Works

The Secret of Integrity and Honor

Just like The Secret of Gratitude and Generosity, these two secrets are separate but function as one. You cannot have integrity without honor or honor without integrity – even though they are different, they operate together.

> *. . .keep away from sexual immorality. . . and that in this matter no one should wrong his brother or take advantage of him . . .Now about brotherly love we do not need to write to you, for you yourselves have been taught by God to love each other. . .Make it your ambition to lead a quiet life, to mind your own business and to work with your hands. . .so that you will not be dependent on anybody.* Excerpts from I Thessalonians 4:3-12 (NIV)

This comes across as just common sense, normal puritan morals, and work ethics, but it is more, so much more. Integrity and Honor are not just ethical activities; they are a heart attitude – a heart motive. It is something God grows in us if we give ourselves over to Him for this purpose.

The Secret of Honor

Set Apart = Sanctified = Holy = Someone of HONOR

To be set apart for His service is to be called Holy. Integrity and honor flow from a heart that has been given to Him. A heart in His hand is holy. If you study the Greek and Hebrew words and see how they are used in the Bible, you will discover that the above statement is absolutely right!

"The opposite of holy is not sinful or evil. The opposite of holy is ordinary."

John Dickson, worship leader, Glory of Zion, Denton, TX

Dr. Robert D. Heidler wrote in his book The Messianic Church Arising! (pg. 120-121):

> *Holiness doesn't mean "free from sin". Holiness means "set apart from the ordinary" or "elevated above the norm." The best one word definition of "holy" is the word "***special"***! To treat something as holy is to honor it as special!*
>
> *We see in the first chapters of Genesis. The first time God called something HOLY was in Genesis 2 when God blessed the seventh day and designated it as "HOLY."*
>
> *Calling the seventh day holy did not mean that the days one through six were worldly, bad, or sinful! The first six days were good days. God said they were very good. But they were not holy. There were just ordinary days. God set the seventh day apart from the rest and said, "This day is SPECIAL."*
>
> *In Leviticus 10, God gave Aaron instructions for serving at the tabernacle. He warned Aaron to be careful to "distinguish between the HOLY and the COMMON." God was saying, "Don't take what is SPECIAL and treat it as ORDINARY!" . . .*

> *Being holy is being "set apart from the ordinary." If something is "holy," it is designated for special purposes and deserving of special treatment. To treat something as HOLY means that you treat it with HONOR.*

If we choose to be, we can be set apart for good works – God works. If we treat our relationship to God as chief, over and above our *ordinary* relationships, then we honor Him, and our life with Him becomes special, HOLY! We all have numerous things going on in our inner life. That is the location for our conscience, imagination, desires, motives, attitudes, thoughts, emotions, purposes, will. To clean up the inner life is an ongoing partnership work with the Holy Spirit. Everything that defiles the heart (inner life) must be presented to the Holy Spirit for processing. We must choose to work with the Holy Spirit to clean up our inner life – it is called dying to what "I" want. We make this out to be hard, but it is simply letting go of what we want and taking what He has for us, which is ALWAYS better. We choose to let Him do the work.

> *Therefore we do not lose heart. Though outwardly we are wasting away, yet inwardly we are being renewed day by day. For our light and momentary troubles are achieving for us an eternal glory that far outweighs them all. So we fix our eyes not on what is seen, but on what is unseen. For what is seen is temporary, but what is unseen is eternal.* II Corinthians 4:16-18 (NIV)

> *Instead, it should be that of your inner self, the unfading beauty of a gentle and quiet spirit, which is of great worth in God's sight.* I Peter 3:4 (NIV)

Holiness is an inner purity, an inner attitude: "*For out of the abundance of the heart the mouth speaketh*" Matthew 12:34 (KJV). I heard Joyce Meyer say on one of her broadcasts, "Inner Purity equals Outer Power." Isn't that our goal? I know I want the Operational Power of God in my life – every minute of every day.

Several years ago I had a bumper sticker (probably the only bumper sticker I have ever had) that said, "Attitudes are contagious, is yours worth catching?" The right attitude comes from inner purity; inner purity comes from a work of the Holy Spirit, which we must allow – a Spirit-to-spirit work. Beloved, The Secret of God is not accomplished through a book of rules or a strict formula, but by a Divine DNA change in our Spirit that infects and changes our soul (heart). Yes, it is contagious – we catch it from God – and we give it to those in our world.

> *Honor your father and your mother, as the LORD your God has commanded you, so that you may live long and that it may go well with you in the land the LORD your God is giving you.* Deuteronomy 5:16 (NIV)

First, it is a commandment, one with a promise – a blessing. Remember, Abraham believed God and it was credited to him as right standing (HOLINESS). Honor is an action that comes from an attitude of the heart. Just like Love or Forgiveness or the other Secrets, it begins as something we choose to be willing to do, but need God's grace to accomplish.

To be dishonorable in any area is an action that disables the purpose and power of the Secret of God. Note, I did not say it stops the power, but it clogs up everything. Worse, it produces dishonor, which will come back on you in greater proportions. Sorry, that's how it works.

> *Simply let your 'Yes' be 'Yes,' and your 'No,' 'No'; anything beyond this comes from the evil one.* Matthew 5:37 (NIV)

Honor is more than being good to your parents or letting your "yes" be "yes" – for example: My body does not does not define who I am. I am not my body, but my body holds me. This is the body God gave me in my Mother's womb – He formed it. This body has been with me from the beginning of me and will be transformed from a physical body into a spiritual body when I am transferred from this realm to the heavenly realm.

Many of us, especially us women, are ashamed of how we look. We look in the mirror and are disgusted with what we see. It occurred to me recently that my attitude of disgust is an act of dishonor and pronounces shame over my life. Shame is an issue I have asked God to expose and heal. Shame is a form of dishonor; dishonor is the opposite of honor. The Bible tells me that with honor comes blessing (see Ephesians 6:2).

A promise I found early in my relationship is one I confess often when shame tries to slip back into my life.

> *Instead of shame and dishonor, you will enjoy a double share of honor. You will possess a double portion of prosperity in your land, and everlasting joy will be yours.* Isaiah 61:7 (NLT)

The whole sixty-first chapter of Isaiah is wonderful. Oh my, how subtle is the deception and how blind have I have often been to the gift of God right in front of me. This precious body has carried me from birth to now. It allowed me to play as a child, pick flowers, and it laid me down in the clover so I could watch the clouds and dream of God. It made me run, dance, swing, sing, and swim. This precious body has been embraced and has embraced others – it has held love. It learned to write, draw, plant, and build.

This precious body has a language and has communicated happiness, fear, love and anger. This precious body produced the lives of two other people – it held and fed them and taught them how to walk, run, talk and sing. This precious body has praised its maker and laughed and wept before Him. I know every area of this body, how it should and should not feel. When it's tired it will continue to work for me, if I ask. Yes, this precious body is my friend, and as much as anything else on this earth it deserves my thanks and my honor.

Next time you look in the mirror or at a photograph – stop – don't turn away; examine it, and thank your body for being your good friend and companion. Then thank God for His precious gift. Shame is not the garment your body was made to wear. Isaiah 61:3 says

> *. . . to bestow on them a crown of beauty instead of ashes, the oil of gladness instead of mourning, and a* ***garment*** *of* ***praise*** *instead of a spirit of despair. They will be called oaks of righteousness, a planting of the LORD for the display of his splendor.*

Honoring yourself or honoring your parents may be a stretch for some of us. However, it is an attitude that our Father God wants us to develop – for all areas of our life; it is an attitude He is ready to impart to us.

Recently in one of the quiet times I spend with Him, He asked me to find my song and to sing it to Him. I do not sing; I cannot read music, and I did not understand what it was He wanted me to do. So I did what I knew – obedience is all He wanted. I sang, off key, but it was genuine. Then He began to open my understanding from various sources that *I am a song*. My life, my attitude is a song that is music to His ears. Our precious Lord God is so very good – the all powerful One who created everything loves us and is interested in calling us "special"!

The Secret of Integrity

> Integrity: *in·teg·ri·ty – the state of being whole, entire, or undiminished.* – Random House Unabridged Dictionary

Integrity is an architectural or a construction term meaning strong, whole and able to stand. Previously when I thought of integrity I thought, "An honest and honorable person; a person of their word." It is, but that is a byproduct – it so much more. It has more to do with strength and stability of character. Character is the foundational core of who we are. This character comes from the healing presence of the relationship we develop with Jesus Christ.

Jesus talks about building our house on the rock so when the storms of life come (and they will) our foundation will stand. That is integrity: stability and strength in good and in hard times. Sometimes it is just as hard to remain stable in times of great abundance as it is in times of lack. He wants us to have the integrity to live well in either situation or all those in between.

> *I know both how to be abased, and I know how to abound: everywhere and in all things I am instructed both to be full and to be hungry, both to abound and to suffer need.* Philippians 4:12 (KJV)

Living in Mississippi I have seen my share of hurricanes, most recently Katrina. My son and daughter-in-law had a home in Waveland, Mississippi, a fully furnished, three-bedroom, two-bath house, one block off the Bay of St. Louis. When the National Guard let them back in to see what was left after the storm, it did not take long – only the foundation stood the test of the storm. All the other stuff of life was gone, swept into the Gulf by the tidal surge.

> *He is like a man which built an house, and digged deep, and laid the foundation on a rock: and when the flood arose, the stream beat vehemently upon that house, and could not shake it: for it was founded upon a rock.* Luke 6:48 (KJV)

Jesus is the rock on which our foundation stands; with Him we have integrity to live above the stuff and storms of life.

OUR WORK – OUR INTEGRITY IN ACTION

I need to add a couple of words about work: WE SHOULD! I am not referring to gaining our salvation or our access to God by doing good works. Salvation cannot be earned through good works; it is a gift of God – paid by Jesus in our behalf at Calvary. Good works are the byproduct of our salvation and our relationship to God.

If you have plenty of money and you don't need a paying job, you still need to work. Sitting around on the telephone all day is NOT ministry. If you are a stay-at-home mom (or dad), clean your house, care for your family; that is your job. If you are retired, serve your community, clean the bathrooms at church, or care for an elderly neighbor's yard. There is a vast list of opportunities that God has for us to seek out and accomplish in the corner of the world where He has placed us. He does not want His people at home just watching television. If you must stay home, become an intercessor. Pray at least five hours per day, every day.

> *. . .nor did we eat anyone's food without paying for it. On the contrary, we worked night and day, laboring and toiling so that we would not be a burden to any of you. . .For even when we were with you, we gave you this rule: If a man will not work, he shall not eat.*
> II Thessalonians 3:8, 10 (NIV)

As Paul traveled throughout the Gentile world, sharing Jesus and His good news, he never went any place with the expectation that he would be taken care of by the people for whom he labored. In the world today there are established jobs in the ministry that are legitimate salaried positions, but not all of us are pastors, music directors, youth ministers, or traveling evangelists. One of the pastor's jobs is to equip the church (us) to do the work of and for Christ (Ephesians 4: 11).

In Genesis 2:15 God gave His first man his first job. *"And the Lord God took the man and put him into the garden of Eden to dress it and to keep it."* According to the Dake Reference Bible, man's assignment was to cultivate and preserve the garden from all intruders. God gave man a job and trusted him to do it well. That tells me that God considers our work important.

Our work should make God known, whether it is at home, church setting, office, school, hospital, or on the road. Our work is not just about making a living; it is about touching our world for Him and establishing His Kingdom, His dominion. We don't do this work by grabbing people by the lapels and getting in their face, by wearing religious t-shirts, or thumping the Bible and quoting scripture. We do this work by BEING His and allowing His life to flow through us. The quality of our work and the character of our lives should express that and draw people to us.

As a Child of God, credibility with the world is essential. The world will not respect you if there is no work (activity) to back up your faith. Beloved, talk is cheap; our neighbors want to see our faith in action. Are we any good to the world around us? Why would anyone want to know our Jesus if all they see in our life is self-centered laziness and a "me and mine" mentality. Enough said.

Integrity and Honor are Spirit-transformed inner attitudes and strengths that manifest credibility and holiness to the world around us. They produce storm-proofing and life-producing power flowing from the core of every believer.

"Heaven's calendar has seven Sundays a week. God sanctifies each day. He conducts holy business at all hours and in all places. He turns the uncommon into the common by turning kitchen sinks into shrines, cafes into convents and nine-to-five work days into spiritual adventures."

Max Lucado

THE TIMOTHY DIRECTIVE

USE YOUR SPIRITUAL GIFT

> *Do not neglect the Spiritual gift within you, which was bestowed on you through prophetic utterance with the laying on of hands by the presbytery.* I Timothy 4: 14 (NAS)

We can be talked out of stepping up to the plate and operating in the Spiritual gifts given to us. Therefore, we must change our minds intentionally, make it believe what the Spirit says and what the Word of God says, not what your enemy says or what you feel.

How do we receive these gifts? In the scripture above Timothy was admonished to not neglect that which was "*bestowed on you through prophetic utterance with the laying on of hands by the presbytery.*" This type of gift is given as an impartation from another who operates in this gift. This impartation does not diminish their gift; it is a download. Prophetic utterance is a living proclamation that empowers us.

> *There are different kinds of gifts, but the same Spirit. There are different kinds of service, but the same Lord. There are different kinds of working, but the same God works all of them in all men. Now to each one the manifestation of the Spirit is given for the common good.*

> *To one there is given through the Spirit the message of wisdom, to another the message of*

> *knowledge by means of the same Spirit, to another faith by the same Spirit, to another gifts of healing by that one Spirit, to another miraculous powers, to another prophecy, to another distinguishing between spirits, to another speaking in different kinds of tongues, and to still another the interpretation of tongues.*
>
> *All these are the work of one and the same Spirit, and he gives them to each one, just as he determines. The body is a unit, though it is made up of many parts; and though all its parts are many, they form one body. So it is with Christ. For we were all baptized by one Spirit into one body—whether Jews or Greeks, slave or free—and we were all given the one Spirit to drink.* I Corinthians 12: 4-13 (NIV)

These are creative gifts deposited in us for our good and the common good. I know people who have, from time to time, operated in all these gifts, because they are open and available to be used by God in the present. Yes, all these gifts are still functioning in the twenty-first century church – at least through those who allow it and believe. These gifts are like the x-ray vision of the fictional Superman. They allow us to SEE into the Spirit realm and PULL what is needed into the physical realm.

What are these gifts? There are nine listed by Paul in I Corinthians 12, which I will list and define briefly. However, there are many wonderful books giving greater details on the purpose and use of these wonderful, supernatural, gifts. Here I will give you the briefest definitions to begin your working knowledge.

These gifts fall into three natural divisions:

1. Gifts of revelation – the mind gifts
   a. <u>The Word of Wisdom.</u> This is supernatural revelation or insight into the divine will and purpose, showing how to solve any problem that may arise.

b. The Word of Knowledge. This is supernatural revelation of divine knowledge or insight in the divine mind, will, or plan; and also the plans of others that man could not know of himself.
c. Discerning of Spirits. This is supernatural revelation or insight into the realm of spirits to detect them and their plans.

2. Gifts of inspiration – vocal gifts
   a. Prophecy. This is supernatural utterance in the native tongue. It is a miracle of divine utterance, not conceived by human thought or reasoning. It includes speaking to men for edification and exhortation and comfort.
   b. Diverse kinds of tongues. This is supernatural utterance in other languages which are not known to the speaker.
   c. The interpretation of tongues. This is simply supernatural ability to interpret in the native tongue what is uttered in other languages not known by the one who interprets by the Spirit.

3. Gifts of Power – working gifts
   a. Faith. This is supernatural ability to believe God without human doubt, unbelief, and reasoning.
   b. The gifts of healing. This is supernatural power to heal all manner of sicknesses without human aid or medicine.
   c. The working of miracles. This is supernatural power to intervene in the ordinary course of nature and to counteract natural laws if necessary.

These gifts enable us to know what to do, when to do it, how to do it, and gives us absolute success in the doing of **IT** – regardless of how things look – before, during and after. These gifts are the software sitting on our operating system, deposited on our hard drive.

We can do all things through Christ who strengthens us (Philippians 4:18).

SHARE THE SECRET

> *Preach the Word; be prepared in season and out of season; correct, rebuke and encourage—with great patience and careful instruction.* II Timothy 4:2 (NIV)

This is quite an exhortation, beloved. Can we accomplish all this? Yes, but we must do it whole and empowered – Spirit to spirit. If we do this under our own strength, we have simply turned back to a religion – rules and duty, without life. You have probably heard it said, "God is not looking for our abilities; He is looking for our availability." He is happy to supply the ability. As a matter of fact, He wants us to operate in His ability – in our weakness, He is made strong.

> *But he said to me, "My grace is sufficient for you, for my power is made perfect in weakness." Therefore I will boast all the more gladly about my weaknesses, so that Christ's power may rest on me.* II Corinthians 12:9 (NIV)

We Christians need to know The Secret power of God in order to overcome the world around us. It is His will for us all to know Him and be empowered by His Spirit. Our family, friends, neighbors, co-workers, and colleagues all need to know Him and the operational power of His secret. Teach and live this secret with patience and careful instruction.

Jesus accomplished many signs and wonders, but He said (we) His disciples would do greater. Everything He did and does through us is done because of His great love. The Secret of God is for His Friend. It is the life-giving, creative deposits that enable us to pull from the supernatural in the natural realm. Most importantly, beloved, the best way to "share the secret" is to live it. Talk is cheap; operational success SCREAMS truth. This will draw people to us and to Him. They will want what we have, physically and spiritually.

> *Neither do men light a candle, and put it under a bushel, but on a candlestick; and it giveth light unto all that are in the house.* Matthew 5:15 (KJV)

I grew up going to church, so I had some basic Biblical knowledge, but as a young adult I began to view it as historical information rather than absolute truth. I believed in the possibility of a God – a God who created the universe, zapped it with life and then left us to our own course of action. This God did not know us personally and certainly did not know or care about me.

As I grew up, I began to look for a sphere of supernatural power. I realized I needed this power to exist successfully in my world. I did not believe it was in Christianity because the Jesus they taught was much too passive to suit me. This quest took me down the road of *the dark side* as George Lucus called it in *Star Wars*. To be sure, I found a degree of power – power without peace, power without hope. I walked through this time of searching knowing there must be more to life than just the living of it.

Fortunately, I found a God who knows us personally and cares about every facet of our lives. Long before there were any of us, He planned us from His heart; He formed us in our mother's womb (Psalm 139); He has numbered the hairs on our head (Matthew 10:30). We are counted as precious to Him – the creator of all that is seen and all that is unseen.

This wonderful God took no offence in my quest, but directed me to walk into a face-to-face encounter with the source of all power – His Son, Jesus Christ. This wonderful God also gave me wonderful, careful, and patient mentors who preached the Word and instructed me in the discipline of my new position in Christ. They were prepared in season and out of season (they let me call them day and night). They lovingly corrected, rebuked, and encouraged me. They taught me The

Secret of God in word and in actions. They encouraged me to develop a Spirit-to-spirit relationship with this wonderful, loving Lord God.

I would be lacking honor for all that has been given to me if I didn't turn around and pour it into you through these pages. I also pray that my wonderful Lord will open the heart (eyes) of your understanding (Ephesians 1:18) and that your spirit, your life, and the world around you will be transformed by this secret.

> *. . . who alone possesses immortality and dwells in* ***unapproachable light****, whom no man has seen or can see To Him be honor and eternal dominion! Amen.* I Timothy 6:16 (NAS)

Provisional Power to Possess

Allow me to wrap this up with a few last words: The Secret of God becomes an operational part of our life by choosing to get ourselves out of the way and deliberately allowing the Holy Spirit to do the necessary work in us. Our spirit must become connected to God during our lifetime, by our choice, and then we must submit to the Holy Spirit to allow these qualities to sprout, grow and produce through the power of His grace. Then we get to become one of those people who walk in the extravagant riches of His miraculous power, are liberated from the bondage of the enemy of God, and acquire the abundant provision (right here and now in this physical realm) that Jesus PROMISED.

There are only two kinds of Christians: Professors and Possessors. I profess the Name of Christ over my life, but that is not enough to truly possess all that name has to offer. I must pursue relationship with the creator over and above securing the name. In that pursuit I gain the power to possess EVERYTHING that name has to offer. Furthermore, with that power I extend our dominion (His Kingdom).

When I married, all that belonged to my husband became mine and all that belonged to me became his. As a Christian, I have become the bride of Christ – all that He is became mine and all that I am became His. As His possession and His bride, I am empowered to take back that which was lost and **occupy** until He comes back to get us (Luke 19:13).

In Him I have faith (positive expectation), love, forgiveness, proper perspective, gratitude, generosity, integrity, honor, and humility all linked together with unity (oneness with Him), fueled by His living Word, **empowered by His Grace (provisional power)**. Nothing, beloved, is lacking; nothing is impossible. What you need, what you have been promised, is then drawn from the Spirit realm into your physical realm. The grace of God is not an excuse to keep living the way we have always lived. It is, beloved, the provisional power to change our ordinary lives into the life He has set aside for us to possess.

Our Father-God has also deposited gifts and creative abilities in us; He desires these gifts to be operational in our life. I am not talking exclusively about spiritual gifts. All creative gifts are from God. Gifts like writing, art (of every medium), music, business, building, dance, design, composing, gardening, entertaining, humor, speaking. . . . . . What are yours? If you're not sure, ask Him to show you and to help you develop them. If you are already operating in your gifts, He will rejoice in helping you refine them.

> *My purpose is that they may be encouraged in heart and united in love, so that they may have the full riches of complete understanding, in order that they may know the mystery (secrets) of God, namely, Christ.* Colossians 2:2 (NIV, emphasis mine)

Jesus Christ is:

The Living Word of God (our fuel)
The Secret of Faith
The Secret of Love
The Secret of Perspective
The Secret of Gratitude and Generosity
The Secret of Integrity and Honor
The Secret of Unity
The Secret of Humility

The Secret of God can be easily translated into any area of life requiring His power to accomplish, overcome or change.

- Addictions (of any kind)
- Weight Loss – Health retention
- The ability to budget and handle finances of any size
- Learning disabilities
- Relationship problems
- Fear and intimidation of any kind
- Anxiety over anything
- Insecurity
- Infirmity
- Shame
- (fill in the blank)___

Simply and finally, the Secret of God is our connection to His Spirit (Spirit to spirit), our submission to the process and the power of His Grace to possess all He has for us that we may be all He created us to be in His world.

THE CREATIVE SEED
(Core Scriptures in Book Order)

Romans 4:17 "Make Something Out of Nothing"
Speaking of Abraham, Paul said. . .it is written: "I have made you a father of many nations." He is our father in the sight of God, in whom he believed—the God who gives life to the dead and calls things that are not as though they were. (NIV)

I Corinthians 4: 1 We are "Trusted Servants"
So then, men ought to regard us as servants of Christ and as those entrusted with the secret things of God. (NIV)

II Corinthians 4: 18 "Our View"
So we fix our eyes not on what is seen, but on what is unseen. For what is seen is temporary but what is unseen is eternal.

Galatians 4: 22-23 "Flesh or Spirit?"
Abraham, remember, had two sons: one by the slave woman and one by the free woman. The son of the slave woman was born by human connivance; the son of the free woman was born by God's promise. This illustrates the very thing we are dealing with now. The two births represent two ways of being in relationship with God. (The Message)

Ephesians 4: 2-3 "Unity"
Be completely humble and gentle; be patient, bearing with one another in love. Make every effort to keep the unity of the Spirit through the bond of peace. (NIV)

Philippians 4: 6
Turn your worry into Worship, your griping into Gratitude. Be anxious for nothing, but in everything by prayer and supplication with thanksgiving let your requests be made known to God. (NAS)

Colossians 4: 6 "Watch your mouth"
Use your heads as you live and work among outsiders. Don't miss a trick. Make the most of every opportunity. Be gracious in your speech. The goal is to bring out the best in others in a conversation, not put them down, and not cut them out. (The Message)

I Thessalonians 4: 3-12 "Sanctification, Love and Work"
. . .keep away from sexual immorality. . . and that in this matter no one should wrong his brother or take advantage of him . . .Now about brotherly love we do not need to write to you, for you yourselves have been taught by God to love each other. . .Make it your ambition to lead a quiet life, to mind your own business and to work with your hands. . .so that you will not be dependent on anybody. (NIV)

I Timothy 4: 14 "Use Your Spiritual Gift"
Do not neglect the Spiritual gift within you, which was bestowed on you through prophetic utterance with the laying on of hands by the presbytery. (NAS)

II Timothy 4:2 "Share This Secret"
Preach the Word; be prepared in season and out of season; correct, rebuke and encourage—with great patience and careful instruction. (NIV)

Hebrews 4: 12 "The Fuel"
For the word of God is living and active and sharper than any two-edged sword, and piercing as far as the division of soul and Spirit, of both joints and marrow, and able to judge the thoughts and intentions of the heart.

(NAS Life Application Bible Study Notes: AUTHOR: Paul, Luke, Barnabas, Apollos, Silas, Philip, Pricilla and others have been suggested because the name of the author is not given in the Biblical text itself. Whoever it was speaks of Timothy as "Brother" (13:23). (I personally believe Paul is the author, therefore, I included it in my reading.)

Homework: Get index-type note cards, look each of these scriptures up in the translated version you prefer, write them on the cards and begin to memorize them. To get to know these scriptures is vital to your complete transformation: Spirit, Soul and Body.

Him in you – ALL things are possible!
~ The End (of the old) ~
~ A New Beginning ~

Linda McClary Martin

CPSIA information can be obtained at www.ICGtesting.com
Printed in the USA
BVOW07s0547210814

363640BV00001B/1/P

9 780981 965734